NEW ZEALAND

WILD FLOWERS HANDBOOK

Owen and Audrey Bishop
Photographs by Nic Bishop

Hodder & Stoughton
A member of the Hodder Headline Group

A catalogue record for this book is available from
The National Library of New Zealand.

Some of the material in this book is adapted from Owen and Nic Bishop's
previous publication, *Wild Flowers of New Zealand*.

ISBN 1-86958-924-6

Cover designed and produced by Hodder Moa Beckett
Cover illustration by Deborah Hinde
Design and typeset by Chris O'Brien
Printed in Hong Kong through Colorcraft Ltd., Hong Kong.

Contents

Owen and **Audrey Bishop** were born in England and were educated at Bristol University. Owen graduated in botany and then researched in plant physiology at the University of Oxford. Audrey too studied botany at Bristol University, as well as chemistry. She researched in chemistry at Oxford and then made her career as a human cytogeneticist at the University of Sheffield. She later established and ran a human genetics diagnostic centre at one of Sheffield's hospitals, the first such unit in Britain. The Bishops travelled extensively while Owen worked for the British Council and as a science education adviser for the United Nations. Between them, they have had over sixty books published, including fifteen on biology and natural history. They first came to New Zealand in 1984 to visit their son Nic. They returned in 1987 to work with Nic on the *Wild Flowers of New Zealand*, subsequently acquiring New Zealand citizenship. They now live in Wellington.

Nic Bishop was born in England in 1955. He completed a BSc in plant science at Nottingham University in 1976, then travelled to New Zealand for a working holiday in 1977. He has remained here ever since, completing a doctorate at Lincoln College, Canterbury, in 1988. He has been a keen photographer since adolescence and has had work featured in numerous conservation publications, calendars and magazines. His first book, *Untouched Horizons*, was published in 1989; it was followed in 1992 by *The Natural History of New Zealand*.

Introduction

This book describes over 300 of the flowering plants that you are most likely to notice while you are out and about in New Zealand. It helps you to find their names, shows you where and when to look for them, and tells you interesting things about them. The book is easy for anyone to use, yet contains enough information to satisfy the enthusiast.

The wild flowers of New Zealand consist of native plants and introduced plants. Most of the native plants are found nowhere else in the world, and have lived here for millions of years.

The introduced plants have been brought to New Zealand from almost all parts of the world, mainly during the nineteenth and twentieth centuries. Many were introduced deliberately, generally from Europe, for cultivation on farms and in gardens, by the early settlers. Since then, they have escaped and have become naturalised on roadsides, on waste land, in scrub or in similar places.

Other plants have been introduced accidentally, as weed seeds in soil attached to commercially imported plants, for example, or as impurities in crop seeds.

Whether introduced deliberately or accidentally, these plants are now a permanent part of the New Zealand scene; they are the ones we notice most often, for they live in areas in and around our settlements. In reserves — both local and national — and other relatively undisturbed places, there is a profusion of native plants waiting to be found and identified. If you go further, to the wilder areas of New Zealand's national parks, you will find many more. This book includes the commonest of the native and introduced plants that you are likely to find — the ones you will see in everyday living and while on holiday.

Finding your way

To help you get quickly to the photograph of the plant you are identifying, the photographs are divided into seven groups and pictorially coded as follows:

Daisy-like flowers
The rays are usually white or yellow, but there are a few with other colours, and we include in this group a few plants that have no rays at all.

Dandelion-like flowers
The dandelion-like flowers have rays but no disc, and all except one in this book are yellow (the exception has blue rays).

Umbrella-like plants
This group has many small flowers (usually white) mounted in flat-topped clusters on stalks that spread out like the spokes of an umbrella.

Cross-shaped flowers
The flowers have four petals, all the same size, and arranged to make a cross. Their petals are distinctive because they are *not* joined to each other. Also the base of each petal is long and narrow, with the wide part spreading out (like the petal shown on p. 111) to form the cross.

Small, inconspicuous flowers
The flowers are too small for you to see exactly what they are like, or they may have only a few greenish or brownish scales instead of petals.

If your plant does not belong to one of the groups above, decide which one of the two following groups it belongs to.

Regular-shaped flowers
The petals are all the same size and colour; they spread out from the centre like the rays of the sun.

Irregular-shaped flowers
The petals are unequal in size, and differ in shape; they may also have different colours.

Describing the plants

Each description begins with information set out like this:

Scientific name (an asterisk * means that the plant is an introduced one) **Common name, or names**	Family name (English equivalent in brackets) Symbols Flower size

What the symbols mean

✔ Used as food
♥ Produces aromatic substances (flavouring, perfumes)
✚ Reputed to have healing properties
m Used by the Maori
✘ Seriously poisonous

The detailed descriptions of each plant follow. These are not intended to be complete botanical descriptions telling you everything about the plant. They are written to help you confirm that the plant you are trying to identify is really the same kind as the one shown in the photograph. So they help to point out the differences between the plant in the photograph and any other common plant that has a similar appearance. If there are any technical words in the descriptions that you do not understand, refer to p. 111.

One feature that is not easy to show precisely in a photograph is the size of the flowers. Sizes of flowers are indicated by figures on the right-hand side of the page, level with the common name. These usually give the flower diameter in millimetres. If flowers vary in diameter, the lower and upper limits are given, for example, '15–25mm' means that the flowers vary in diameter from 15mm to 25mm. For a few species, the length of the flower is easier to measure, and we quote the length followed by 'long', for example, '50mm long'.

The height of mature plants is indicated by using standard descriptions:

Height	Description
Up to 100 mm	low
100 to 300mm	short
300 to 600mm	medium
Over 600mm	tall

Some kinds of plant span more than one height group; for these plants we use terms such as 'medium to tall', meaning that plants range in height from 300mm to over 600mm.

The description may also mention other similar plants, pointing out how they differ. The following paragraph describes the plant's regional distribution throughout New Zealand, what kinds of places it lives in, and during what part of the year you are likely to find it flowering. If you check that your plant is supposed to grow where you found it, and supposed to be flowering on the date you found it, this helps to confirm that you have identified it correctly. Plants may be found in flower slightly earlier than the specified dates in northern areas or in sheltered places and they may be in flower slightly later in southern areas.

Where space permits the description may be followed by interesting points about the uses or history of the plant or its relatives.

Finding a description or photograph

Sometimes you may want to look up the description or photograph of a plant of which you already know the name.

When you know the common name use the index (p. 109) to find its entry in the book. The common names are listed alphabetically, with page numbers. If there are several different plants with the same basic common name, such as black orchid, Easter orchid, greenhood orchid (and several others), they are all indexed under the one entry, in this case 'Orchids', with page numbers.

When you know its scientific name, decide which of the seven pictorially coded groups (pages 5–6) it is in. The plants are listed alphabetically in each group by scientific name.

Daisy-like flowers

*Achillea millefolium**
Yarrow

Asteraceae (Daisy Family)
✔ ✚ up to 10mm

A short to medium, hairy, perennial plant with creeping rhizome and erect, furrowed, woolly stems. It emits a strong aromatic smell when crushed. The two-pinnate leaves are dark green and finely divided, the segments being partly divided pinnately, which gives the plant a feathery appearance. It has a flat-topped inflorescence and can be mistaken for one of the umbrella plants (p. 23). But each 'flower' is really a flower-head consisting of about 20 tubular disc flowers and about five ray flowers with short, off-white or pinkish rays.

It grows in grassy places, often surviving the lawn-mower as a low-growing plant on lawns. Yarrow flowers from December to May.

The name 'yarrow' comes from the Greek *hiera*, 'holy herb'. This plant is named after the hero of Greek legends, Achilles, who used it to heal the wounds of his soldiers. This is not recommended since it causes inflammation if the wound is subsequently exposed to sunlight. Young yarrow leaves may be eaten in salads.

*Anthemis cotula**
Stinking mayweed

Asteraceae (Daisy Family)
15–30mm

A short to medium, annual herb with a very unpleasant smell. The leaves are similar to those of yarrow, though not as feathery. The solitary flower-heads have 8–21 white rays, turning back as the flower-head matures. The very narrow, sharply pointed scales between the flowers distinguish it from the rare corn chamomile (*A. arvensis**) and from chamomile (*Chamaemelum nobile**) in which the scales are spear-shaped. In chamomile, the tips of the scales are rounded, while in corn chamomile they are pointed.

It grows on roadsides, in pastures, lawns, and waste places, and flowers from December to March.

This weed was unpopular in the days of hand harvesting, as its juices cause blisters on the skin.

Arctotheca calendula*
Cape weed

Asteraceae (Daisy family)
35–60mm

A low to short, spreading, felted or hairy annual, with a basal rosette of pinnately cut leaves. The end segment of the leaf is larger than the other segments, as shown in the photograph. Flower-heads are solitary, with four or five rows of greenish bracts. The rays are tinged with green or purple underneath and their tips have three teeth. The pappus consists of a row of 4–8 dry scales.

Cape weed grows on roadsides, beaches and waste areas, being common on verges and as a weed in lawns. It flowers from October to April.

The name 'Cape weed' refers to its original introduction from South Africa.

Arctotis stoechadifolia*
Arctotis

Asteraceae (Daisy Family)
70–100mm

A short to medium, trailing, silvery white perennial with toothed or pinnately cut leaves. If the leaves are pinnately cut, the terminal segment is much larger than the others. The flower-heads are large and showy in a wide range of colours, including a rich yellow-orange (illustrated), a deep pinkish purple, brick red, and purple. The rays have three teeth at their tips. The disc is blackish purple, and there are five rows of thin, dry, brownish bracts.

It is commonly grown in gardens, often escaping and establishing itself in waste areas, on banks and on roadsides. It flowers from November to March, and outside this period in sunny situations.

This plant is a good example of the strange ways in which some plants are given their scientific names. The name *Arctotis* means 'bear's-ear' and refers to the stiff brown pappus scales on the fruits, which are said to look like a bear's ear. The species name *stoechadifolia* is derived in an even more roundabout way. It means 'Stoechad-like leaves'. This refers to a species of lavender with very similar leaves, which grows on the Stoechades, a group of islands off the south coast of France.

Bellis perennis*
Daisy

Asteraceae (Daisy Family)
20mm

A low, perennial plant with a basal rosette of broad, spoon-shaped leaves, and solitary flower-heads. The rays are often tipped with red, especially on the outside.

It grows in waste areas, lawns and pastures, flowering from September to March.

The 'day's-eye' flower closes at night or in bad weather. The name *Bellis* is from the Latin *bellus*, meaning 'pretty'. The small size of the plant led people to believe that it would make other things small: in years gone by, daisy roots were boiled in milk and fed to puppies to keep them small!

The celmisias

This genus is confined to Australasia and almost all of its 60 or more species are native to New Zealand. Most grow in sub-alpine to high-alpine regions. Identifying celmisias is difficult, as so many of them look alike at first glance, and there are many natural hybrids.

The leaves vary in size, but are usually simple in outline and very often narrow, with a soft, white covering of short hairs, at least on the undersides and sometimes above as well.

There are two main forms of celmisia:

• Short, perennial herbs with leaves in rosettes at the base of the stems. *C. spectabilis* belongs to this group.

• Low-growing shrubs, with leaves closely packed and overlapping each other *along* the stems, or in rosettes at the *ends* of the stems. An example is the white cushion daisy (*C. sessiliflora*) which forms cushions up to 1 metre in diameter. Leaves are covered with short white hairs on both surfaces. The flower-heads (10–20mm) have very short stalks, so that they are level with the tips of the branches.

Celmisia spectabilis
Tikuma, Puakaito, Puheretaiko, Cotton daisy

Asteraceae (Daisy Family)
30–50mm

A short, perennial herb with tough, leathery leaves, hairless and shiny on the upper side, covered with a thick, buff-coloured felt of hairs on the underside. This species is the most widespread of the celmisias, and is found in grassland, tussock and fellfield from 300m to 1700m. It flowers in December and January.

The spectacular flowers give this species its name, *spectabilis*.

Cotula coronopifolia
Bachelor's buttons, Buttonweed

Asteraceae (Daisy Family)
10mm

A low to short, hairless, mat-forming annual, with fleshy stems. It has a camphor-like aromatic smell. The leaves are fleshy, alternate, their bases forming a cup around the stem. The flower heads are solitary, with very short-rayed outer flowers, making it appear as if all the flowers are tubular. The flowers of the related species *C. australis*, Soldier's buttons, are pale yellow, compared with the bright yellow flowers of *C. coronopifolia*. The leaves of *C. australis* are less finely divided; it has hairy leaves and stems.

It grows in relatively wet areas of waste land, especially on or near the coast and around lagoons and swamps. *C. australis* is widely distributed in waste areas, not necessarily in wet situations. Both species flower all the year round.

The name *Cotula* comes from Greek, meaning 'little cup', which refers to the bases of the lower leaves forming a little cup around the stem.

Erigeron karvinskianus*
Mexican daisy

Asteraceae (Daisy Family)
15–25mm

A short , perennial herb with branching leafy, ridged stems. The lower stem leaves are often three-lobed but the other leaves are entire. The flower-heads are daisy-like in appearance and size. Ray flowers may be white, pink, purplish pink, or purple. The pappus consists of a row of long hairs.

Mexican daisy is found in waste areas, streamsides or scrub, often growing on banks. It flowers from September to May. *Erigeron* comes from Greek, meaning 'early/old man' and refers to the whitish, hairy appearance of the flower-heads, seen rather early in the season. This plant is a garden escape which has now become widely naturalised. *Erigeron* and *Bellis* belong to a sub-division of the Asteraceae which includes *Aster*, after which the whole family is named. Aster has many species grown for their showy flowers, especially the well known Michaelmas daisy.

Galinsoga parviflora*
Galinsoga, Gallant soldiers

Asteraceae (Daisy Family)
3–7mm

A short to tall, branching annual with clusters of flower-heads at the tips of the stems. There are up to five rays on each flower-head, and these are small and white. Leaves are opposite and simple, with toothed margins. Pappus scales are broad, with rounded tips.

It grows in disturbed soil, such as gardens and other cultivated areas.

The fruits formed by the disc flowers are topped with a pappus of large, broad scales up to 2.5mm long, which helps the fruits to be scattered by the wind. The fruits formed by the ray flowers have no pappus scales or only small ones, and are not blown far. This is thought to give the plant a chance to spread widely if suitable areas are within its range, but, if not, to increase the number of plants growing close to the parent.

A similar though less common species is *G. quadriradiata**, which has narrow pappus scales with sharply pointed tips.

Gazania linearis*
Gazania

Asteraceae (Daisy Family)
70–100mm

A short to medium perennial with leaves tufted at the ends of rhizomes. The dead leaves remain attached to the plant. The leaves are narrow and lance-shaped, dark green above and felted white below, except on the mid-rib; a few leaves may be pinnate toward the tip. The flower-heads are solitary, on stalks 200–300mm long, and their yellow or orange rays with the basal black patch, spotted white in the centre, make this an easy genus to identify. The black patch may be lacking in some varieties.

This successful escapee from the garden grows on waste areas, cliffs, sand dunes and stream-banks. It flowers from November to February.

A related species, *G. rigens**, has similar flowers with orange rays, and a white-spotted black patch. It has trailing stems ending in tufts of leaves, shorter (50–100mm) flower-stems, and its dead leaves fall off.

Helichrysum bellidioides
Helichrysum

Asteraceae (Daisy Family)
14–22mm

A low to short, perennial herb with spreading, rooting stems and also erect stems which each bear a solitary flower-head. The flowers are all tubular and there are no ray-flowers. Instead, the bracts around the flower-head are long and spreading, so that they look like white rays. They are stiff and membranous in texture, persisting after the flower-heads are dead.

It occurs in a range of open places, at altitudes ranging from lowland to alpine. It flowers from October to March.

The genus name *Helichrysum* comes from the Greek *helios* (the sun), and *chryson* (golden). Such a name is fully justified in the strawflower (*H. bracteatum**), which has large (25–50mm diameter) flower-heads with conspicuous, stiff, golden bracts, spreading out like the rays of the sun. But the flowers of *H. bellidioides* are more like those of the daisy (*Bellis*), and its species name means 'daisy-like'.

Leucanthemum vulgare*
Oxeye daisy, Moon daisy

Asteraceae (Daisy Family)
30–60mm

A short to tall, slightly hairy perennial with entire, dark green leaves, the lower leaves with long stalks, the upper leaves with none, clasping the stem. The margins of the leaves are irregularly toothed. The large, solitary, daisy-like flower-heads make this species easy to identify, though at first glance it may be mistaken for *Anthemis cotula* (p. 8), which has feathery leaves. The only other possible confusion is with the garden-escape, Shasta daisy (*Leucanthemum maximum**), which has larger flower-heads (70–120mm diameter). The leaf margins of the Shasta daisy have teeth of regular size and spacing.

It grows in grassy places and in other waste areas, in grassland and at the margins of forests, flowering from August to May.

This is an attractive and conspicuous plant of the roadside verges. To send someone this flower means 'be patient!' In Europe this plant is usually known as marguerite, a name that is given to another species, *Argyranthemum frutescens*, in New Zealand.

Osteospermum fruticosum *
Dimorphotheca

Asteraceae (Daisy Family)
40–70mm

A short, straggling or mat-forming perennial with fleshy leaves. The flower-heads are solitary. The rays are white on the upper surface, but bluish-mauve below. The relatively small disc, of bluish-purple flowers, often appearing almost black, is a distinctive feature of this plant.
The plant is often grown in gardens and has frequently escaped. It has become widely naturalised on banks and cliffs, especially near the coast. *Osteospermum fruticosum* flowers from August to January.

The raoulias

There are 20 species of *Raoulia* native to New Zealand. Their flower-heads are short-stalked or lacking in stalks. The bracts surrounding the flower-heads are often white or yellow and have a papery texture. In many species the flower-heads are inconspicuous, but in several others the outer bracts are long and showy, like those of a typical daisy. Several of the raoulias form firm, rounded cushions, 500mm or more in diameter, often greyish in colour.

Raoulia grandiflora
Raoulia

Asteraceae (Daisy Family)
up to 15mm

A low cushion-forming or mat-forming, silvery-grey perennial; cushions are up to about 150mm in diameter. The stems are closely covered with small, overlapping leaves, up to 10mm long. The flower-heads are on short stalks, level with the 'surface' of the cushion or mat. The flower-heads are surrounded by spreading, papery, white-tipped bracts looking like ray petals.
This raoulia grows on rocks and fellfield from 1000m to 1900m. It flowers from November to January.
The related species *R. youngii* is similar in appearance, but its leaves are densely covered with a white to pale buff felt and the plant forms very soft snow-white to buff mats. Its leaves are not more than 5mm long.

Senecio elegans *
Purple groundsel

Asteraceae (Daisy Family)
20–40mm

A low to medium, hairless or slightly hairy annual, with leaves pinnately lobed, the lobes often being pinnate again, as in the photograph. Upper stem leaves have short stalks, or none at all, in which case the leaves may clasp the stem. The flower-heads have 11–16 supplementary bracts (see the general description of senecios on p. 16), 2–5mm long, and a single row of 13–14 inner bracts, 5–9mm long. The disc is yellow, but the 12–17 ray flowers are unusual for this genus in being purple, or sometimes pink, purplish pink or white.

It grows on sand dunes and on other coastal sites, though it is sometimes found inland, growing in waste areas. It flowers from August to May.

Senecio jacobaea *
Ragwort

Asteraceae (Daisy Family)
✗ 15–25mm

A medium to tall, biennial or perennial plant. The stems have a downy covering at first, but this clears, leaving the stems hairless. Young plants have a basal rosette of leaves, which usually die away before flowering. The leaves are pinnately lobed, covered with a light web of hairs, the end lobe being small and blunt. Leaf bases clasp the stem. Flower-heads are in more or less flat-topped clusters. The rays of the 11–13 ray flowers are erect at first, then spreading. There are 3–10 supplementary bracts (see the general description of senecios on p.16), 1.5–3mm long. The 11–14 inner bracts are 3–5mm long, with dark brown tips. The fruit bears a pappus of hairs.

Ragwort grows in waste areas, pasture (especially if it is over-grazed), grassy places, and roadsides. It flowers from November to April.

The plant is poisonous to stock and is listed as a noxious plant. The name of the genus is derived from the Latin, *senex*, which means 'old man', referring to the beard-like whitish pappus on the fruits.

The senecios

This is one of the largest plant genera worldwide. There are 34 species of *Senecio* growing wild in New Zealand, 18 of them native. The New Zealand members of the genus are mostly herbs, though some become woody at the base and two are small shrubs. They have alternate leaves, usually simple but often pinnately lobed. There is one row of free inner bracts around each flower-head, but outside of these there may also be a few smaller, supplementary bracts. The number of free and supplementary bracts quoted in the descriptions are typical but plants may occasionally be found with fewer or more bracts. Flowers are usually yellow, and fruits usually have a hairy pappus.

Senecio lautus   Asteraceae (Daisy Family)
Shore groundsel   10–20mm

A low, spreading, hairless or slightly hairy, annual or perennial plant. The leaves are fairly fleshy and divided pinnately into lobes or teeth, about three to six on each side of the mid-stem leaves. There are 6–16 supplementary bracts, 1–3mm long, and 10–13 inner bracts, 4–6.5mm long. The flower-heads have 7–13 ray flowers, with relatively short rays, 2–7mm long.

It lives in coastal areas on cliffs, beaches and rocks, flowering throughout the year.

Senecio skirrodon*   Asteraceae (Daisy Family)
Gravel groundsel   15–30mm

A short to medium annual (sometimes living for a few years), completely hairless except possibly for a few hairs on the mid-veins and bases of the leaves. The leaves are light green, narrow or spear-shaped, with slightly toothed margins. Some leaves may be cut pinnately into three to five sections on each side. Flower-heads are solitary or few in loose clusters. There are 9–17 narrow supplementary bracts, 2–3mm long, and 18–23 narrow inner bracts, 5–7mm long. The bright golden-yellow ray and disc flowers are distinctive.

Gravel groundsel grows in coastal areas and waste places. It flowers in December and January.

*Senecio vulgaris**
Groundsel

Asteraceae (Daisy Family)
✗ 4–5mm

A low to short annual, often covered with cob-web-like hairs, except on the upper surface of the leaves. The flower-heads are nearly always without rays, in loose clusters. It has 8–21 triangular or spear-shaped, black-tipped supplementary bracts, 1–1.25mm long, and 18–21 long, narrow inner bracts, 5.5–8mm long, also with black-pointed tips. The pappus on the ripe fruit forms a prominent spherical 'clock'.

This is very common in a wide range of waste places and disturbed areas, and a frequent weed of gardens and other cultivated land. It flowers all the year round.

The seeds of this most successful weed germinate readily when exposed to light; if covered by soil, only about 15 per cent of seeds will germinate. Living seeds remain in the soil for years, without germinating, until the soil is disturbed and the seeds are exposed to light. The name 'groundsel' comes from the mediaeval name grundeswyle, which means 'earth glutton'.

NOTE: Some species of *Senecio* have inconspicuous flowers. Photographs of these appear in a later section (pp. 39–40).

Dandelion-like flowers

Cichorium intybus *
Chicory

Asteraceae (Daisy Family)
✔ ♥ 35mm

A medium to tall perennial with lower leaves toothed to pinnately lobed, upper leaves simple, margins coarsely toothed, bases clasping the stem. The flower-heads are large and sky-blue in colour. The plant does not have latex.

Chicory grows on roadsides and on waste land, flowering from December to March.

The flowers open from about 8am until noon. The blanched hearts of this plant are sold as 'chicory' and eaten in salads. The roots of chicory, when dried and ground, are used as a coffee substitute and for blending with coffee to modify its flavour. The leaves of the related species *C. endivia* are sold as 'endive' and eaten as a salad vegetable.

Crepis capillaris *
Hawksbeard

Asteraceae (Daisy Family)
10–15mm

A short to medium, hairy annual or biennial with a branching stem. The leaves are shiny, some in the basal rosette, others on the stem. Basal leaves have stalks and may be toothed, but are usually deeply cut into pinnate segments, the segments being directed back toward the leaf base; they are 50–200mm long, 10–30mm wide. Upper leaves are narrower, less deeply cut, stalkless, and have bases that clasp the stem with arrow-shaped points. Outer flowers often have a pink or reddish stripe beneath. The outer surfaces of bracts have short, white hairs and a few dark, glandular hairs. The inner surfaces are hairless.

Hawksbeard is found in a wide range of disturbed habitats, including roadsides and gardens. It flowers from September to March.

Beaked hawksbeard (*C. vesicaria* *) has hairs on both outer and inner surfaces of the bracts, rather larger flowers and leaves (100–200mm long, 40–80mm wide).

The hawkweeds

These are a distinctive sub-group of the dandelion-like plants, and there are hundreds of different forms (microspecies), which are extremely difficult to identify. The main features of the group are: unbranched stems bear a few (or no) leaves, and end in a branching cluster of flower-heads or a single flower-head; flower-heads are nearly always yellow; leaves are spear-shaped, alternate, with toothed margins. *H. praealtum* is a typical hawkweed.

Hieracium praealtum *   Asteraceae (Daisy Family)
King devil   10–25mm

A short to medium, hairy, perennial plant producing runners, by which it spreads rapidly. The leaves of the basal rosette are bluish green in colour, with coarse hairs 2–4mm long, usually on both surfaces. The leaf is lance-shaped, entire or slightly toothed. There are no leaves, or possibly only one or two small leaves, on the stems. The stem is branching, bearing a cluster of 10–25 flower-heads.

It is found in both islands but is more widespread in the South Island, growing in waste places, by roadsides and in scrub. It flowers from November to March.

Hypochoeris glabra *   Asteraceae (Daisy Family)
Smooth catsear   12–15mm

A low to short annual, usually with shiny, hairless leaves. Most of the leaves are in the basal rosettes, with only a few scale-like leaves on the stem, topped by a single flower-head. Flower-heads open only in full sunlight, and the bracts are about the same length as the rays. They enlarge at fruiting, forming a narrow, conical fruiting head. The catsears are easily confused with the hawkbits (*Leontodon* species). To distinguish them, rub a flower-head between your palms to separate the flowers: catsears have narrow yellowish scales among the flowers; hawkbits have none.

Smooth catsear lives in grassy places, sand dunes, rocky and stony places, roadsides and waste land. It flowers from November to May.

19

Lapsana communis *
Nipplewort

Asteraceae (Daisy Family)
✦ 10–20mm

A short to tall, hairy annual with a branching stem, each branch ending in a finely branched cluster of flower-heads. The stem bears several oval leaves, which are often pinnate near the base, ending in a large oval lobe. Upper leaves are undivided but toothed, and the fruits have no hairy pappus. The plant does not have latex.

It lives beside tracks and roads, particularly under trees and bushes. Flowering is from December to March.

The ancient Doctrine of Signatures stated that any plant part that resembles a part of the human body may be used to cure disorders or diseases of that part. The flower buds of nipplewort are shaped similarly to the human nipple and so the plant was thought to cure soreness of the nipples. The ending '-wort' is commonly used for plants that were used as cures, as in toothwort, navelwort and ragwort.

Leontodon taraxacoides *
Lesser hawkbit

Asteraceae (Daisy Family)
12–20mm

A low to medium perennial with a basal rosette and an unbranched, leafless stem ending in a single flower-head; the flower-heads are nodding when in bud. Lesser hawkbit is sometimes confused with dandelion (*Taraxacum*), but its flower-head is smaller and its leaves are only shallowly lobed. The outer rays are greyish on the outside. The pappus on the fruit forms a spherical 'clock' .

This plant may also be confused with the catsears (*Hypochoeris* species). The best way to distinguish them is to take a flower-head and rub it between your palms to separate the flowers. The catsears have yellowish scales among the flowers, but there are none in the hawkbits.

Lesser hawkbit grows in a wide range of habitats, including lawns, swamps, sand dunes and gravel. It flowers from November to April.

The related autumn hawkbit (*L. autumnale* *) differs in having a branched stem, bearing many small leaf-like bracts, especially towards the top. Its flower-heads are erect in bud.

Picris echioides *
Bristly ox-tongue

Asteraceae (Daisy Family)
20–25mm

A medium annual or biennial with bristly hairs on the stem, leaves and bracts. The leaves have prominent hairs and white blister-like swellings which give the plant its common name. On the stem and leaves, the tips of the hairs branch to form three to four hooks. The flowers are pale yellow, sometimes with a red stripe on the outer surface of each ray. They are surrounded by broad, sepal-like, spreading hairy bracts.

It grows on waste land and cultivated land, flowering from January to March.

Picris, together with *Cichorium, Crepis, Hieracium, Hypochoeris, Lapsana, Leontodon, Sonchus* and *Taraxacum*, are all relatives of *Lactuca*, the lettuce plant. They all have a basal rosette of leaves (broad and edible in the lettuce). A milky latex exudes from the cut ends of leaves and stems. Flower-heads of this group consist entirely of ligulate flowers, which are usually yellow.

Sonchus asper *
Prickly sow thistle

Asteraceae (Daisy Family)
20–25mm

A short to medium annual or biennial, usually green or bluish green in colour. Its leaves are lance-shaped, shiny on the upper surface and with wavy, spiny margins. The spines are stiff and prickly compared with those of *S. oleraceus*. The bases of the leaves closely clasp the stem, with rounded lobes.

It lives on waste land, roadsides, pasture, and in gardens. It also grows in sandy, coastal places. Flowers from October to March.

Sow thistles are to be found growing in almost all parts of the world: such genera are said to be pandemic. Genera and species which are found only in very restricted areas are described as being endemic. Having been isolated by the oceans for vast periods of time, New Zealand is particularly rich in endemic species. Many of its plants are found nowhere else in the world. For example, of the 32 species of *Senecio* living wild in New Zealand, 12 are endemic.

21

Sonchus oleraceus*
Sow thistle, Puha

Asteraceae (Daisy Family)
✔ 20–25mm

A short to tall annual, greyish in colour compared with *S. asper*. Its leaves are pinnately lobed, almost to the midrib, the end lobes being largest. The edges of the leaves are toothed, with small spines, but the spines are softer than those of *S. asper*. The leaves have pointed lobes, loosely clasping the stem.

Puha lives on waste land, roadsides, grassland, dunes and beaches, in gardens and even in small cracks in paths and walls. It flowers from November to January.

In the Middle Ages, this plant was cooked and eaten as a vegetable, and is still eaten by some New Zealanders today.

Taraxacum officinale*
Dandelion, Tohetake

Asteraceae (Daisy Family)
✔ ♥ 35–50mm

A low to short perennial, with a basal rosette of deeply toothed and jagged leaves. The stem is single and hollow, with a single flower-head. The yellow rays are usually coloured violet-grey outside, and the bracts curl back. This plant is well known for its conspicuous dandelion 'clocks'.

Dandelion grows on roadsides and waste areas, in pasture, grassland and gardens, and on lawns. It flowers from September to May.

The native dandelion (*T. magellanicum*) is smaller. The bracts are thin, with white margins, not curling back. It lives in mountain areas, from 500m to 1900m.

The name 'dandelion' comes from the French *dent-de-lion*, referring to the jagged 'lion's teeth' of the leaves. The leaves can be eaten, and are rich in vitamin A and iron. The flowers are used for dandelion wine. The roots may be eaten also and can be roasted and ground to make a coffee substitute. This plant, like several others in the Daisy Family, sets its seeds without fertilisation so that cross-fertilisation is impossible. One result of this is that there are hundreds of slightly different types of dandelion, each breeding true.

Umbrella-like plants

Aciphylla colensoi
Wild spaniard

Apiaceae (Carrot Family)
5mm

A tall, robust perennial forming large tufts. The leaves are about 300–500mm long, with two to four pairs of leaflets, having strongly toothed margins and ending in sharp spines. Each leaf has two stipules, also ending in spines. The midribs of the leaflets are stout, and coloured reddish orange or yellow. The inflorescence is up to 2.5m long, with scented flowers in small, dense umbels. Sepals and petals are small. Petals are yellow. The lower bracts of the inflorescence taper to sharp spines.

Lives in the South Island, in grassland, herbfield, and snow tussock herbfield, from 900m to 1500m. Spaniard flowers from November to February.

There are 40 species of *Aciphylla* (meaning 'sharp leaf') in New Zealand, several of the species being as large or larger than *A. colensoi*. Most have the typical 'jointed' leaves and many have long, needle-sharp spines that can cause painful injuries.

Anisotome haastii
Pinakitere

Apiaceae (Carrot Family)
7–9mm

A medium, robust perennial with two- to four-pinnate leaves, 150–250mm long and 60–120mm wide. Leaf segments are narrow, ending in hair-like tips. The leaves are 'flat', the segments lying in one plane. Stalks of the leaves and bracts have prominent sheathing bases. The inflorescence consists of many compound umbels, 50–80mm in diameter, with bracts ending in hair-like tips.

Pinakitere grows in scrub and snow tussock herbfields from 600m to 1500m, flowering from October to February.

There are 16 species of *Anisotome* native to New Zealand, possibly more.

Apium prostratum var. *filiforme*
Tutaekoau, Maori celery

Apiaceae (Carrot Family)
✔ ♥ 1–2mm

A short, spreading to upright perennial, its stems do not take root. Leaves are one-pinnate, the segments being divided into rounded lobes, and the lower leaves often consisting of only three segments. In the variety *prostratum*, the segments of the leaflet are longer and narrower. In the variety *denticulatum*, the leaflets are more divided and the segments have fine toothed edges. In all varieties, the umbels have short (or no) stalks, located opposite the leaves, but there are no bracts or bracteoles.

It is found in coastal areas, growing on rocks, gravel or mud.

This is one of two common plants gathered by Captain Cook in 1796 to prevent scurvy, a common disease of seamen caused by a lack of vitamin C. Freshly collected tutaekoau was a rich source of the vitamin.

Leaves and stems may be eaten; the seeds are used as flavouring. Make sure that you have identified the plant correctly, as it is possible to confuse it with other members of the family, such as the poisonous *Conium maculatum*. Varieties of *A. graveolens** are eaten as celery.

*Conium maculatum**
Hemlock, Mother die

Apiaceae (Carrot Family)
✘ 2mm

A tall, unpleasant-smelling, annual or biennial plant with noticeable reddish purple spots on the stems. The hairless leaves are soft and feathery, being two- to four-pinnate. Bracts taper evenly to a narrow point and are bent back toward the stem. Bracteoles are similar in shape, but smaller, and turned only slightly downward; they are present only on the outsides of the sub-umbels.

A very common plant of waste areas and forest margins, it flowers from September to January.

All parts of this plant are very poisonous, particularly the seeds, since it contains the alkaloid coniine. In ancient Greece a lethal concoction made from the seeds was used to facilitate the death sentence. It is thought that the philosopher Socrates was executed in this fashion.

Daucus carota*
Wild carrot

Apiaceae (Carrot Family)
1–7mm

A medium to tall annual or biennial with three-pinnate, hairy leaves. The bracts of the inflorescence are large and pinnate, with narrow, pointed segments. The bracts and stalks of the umbels curl inward when the inflorescence is young, for a while the stalks straighten, but they curl inward again as the seeds ripen. The flowers are white, but there may be a few reddish or blackish purple flowers in the middle of each umbel. The spines on the fruits are a distinctive feature.

It grows on waste areas, beside roads, on cultivated land and in weedy gardens: flowers from August to May.

This is the wild form of the cultivated carrot. Two other members of this family, parsnip and celeriac, also have edible swollen roots. The family includes many that provide flavourings for the kitchen, including parsely, fennel, dill, chervil, sweet Cicely and lovage. The fruits of another relative, angelica, are used as flavouring in vermouth and in Chartreuse liqueurs; its stems are crystallised with sugar and used as cake decoration. See fennel for more flavourings.

Foeniculum vulgare*
Fennel

Apiaceae (Carrot Family)
✔ ♥ ✚ 1–2mm

A tall perennial with a strong 'liquorice-like' smell. The three- to five-pinnate leaves are finely divided into thread-like segments. The plant is greyish green in colour. The flowers are yellow and there are no bracts on the umbels.

Fennel grows in waste areas, beside roads, on coastal cliffs. It flowers from November to May.

The leaves of fennel are used as a vegetable, and its roots can be grated into a salad. Like many other members of the family, including caraway, cumin, coriander, anise and celery, its fruits are used as flavouring. At one time fennel was used by the Chinese and Hindus to treat snake-bites and scorpion-bites. The Romans made its leaves into wreaths, as an emblem of flattery. It was also believed that placing fennel in a keyhole would keep a house free from ghosts.

Cross-shaped flowers

Brassica rapa*
Wild turnip

Brassicaceae (Mustard Family)
✔ 20mm

A tall annual or biennial with bright green, pinnately lobed lower leaves. The upper leaves are narrowly triangular, their bases clasping the stem. The flowers are in a flat-topped spike. The fruit is a long narrow pod.

Wild turnip grows in pastures, gardens, roadsides and waste areas, flowering from September to February. The cultivated varieties of the turnip are important as food crops. This genus includes the species *B. oleracea* which has a large number of varieties, many of them grown as vegetables (cabbage, cauliflower, brussels sprouts, broccoli, calabrese, kale, kohl rabi and red cabbage). Rape seed (*B. napus*) is widely grown as a field crop for its oil, and as fodder. Mustard (*B. nigra*) is extensively cultivated for making into the condiment, and also for mustard oil; it provides the English name for the family.

Capsella bursa-pastoris*
Shepherd's purse

Brassicaceae (Mustard Family)
2–3mm

A low to medium annual or biennial with toothed, serrated or entire leaves in a basal rosette. The stem leaves are spear-shaped and clasp the stem. The flowers are clustered at the top of the inflorescence, with the heart-shaped pods below.

It lives on waste and cultivated land and flowers most abundantly from September to January, but can be found in flower all the year round.

This plant is also known as 'pickpocket' and 'pickpurse' because it robs the farmer of nutrients in the soil. It is a very successful and pandemic (p. 21) weed, rated as one of the five most abundant plant species in the world. One reason why shepherd's purse is so successful is that its seeds remain alive in the soil for several years, a few germinating each year. In this way it persists in an area for many years once a plant has grown there.

Cardamine debilis
Bittercress

Brassicaceae (Mustard Family)
3–4mm

A short to medium perennial with a shiny green, hairless stem. The leaves are pinnate, thin, and slightly hairy. Basal leaves usually die back after the plant has fruited, their bases remaining. The leaflets are rounded, the end leaflet being a little larger than the others, of which there are one or two pairs. The leaflets have distinctly pointed lobes (note that the leaf at the bottom left of the photograph does *not* belong to this plant), and are not quite symmetrical at the base. The pods spread out almost at right-angles to the stem (compare with *C. hirsuta*, in which they are more erect, often close against the stem, as shown in the photograph).

It lives mainly in forests, from lowland to subalpine areas: flowers from October to January.

Cardamine hirsuta*
Hairy bittercress

Brassicaceae (Mustard Family)
3–4mm

A low to short annual with a basal rosette of pinnate leaves. In spite of its species name, *hirsuta*, which means 'hairy', its stem has no hairs and its leaves are only slightly hairy on their upper surfaces. There are two or three pairs of lobed leaflets on each basal leaf, the leaflets being slightly larger toward the end of the leaf. Stem leaves are similar, though with slightly narrower leaflets. The pods are long and erect (compare with *C. debilis*), over-topping the flowers.

It grows in waste areas, and flowers from August to December.

A comparable plant is wavy bittercress (*C. flexuosa**),which grows in similar, though usually damper, places than hairy bittercress. It is usually a biennial and is noted for its wavy stems, which are hairy at the base. Its leaves are in a basal rosette, with four to six pairs of leaflets. The pods are more or less erect but do not over-top the flowers.

Diplotaxis muralis *
Wall rocket

Brassicaceae (Mustard Family)
8–15mm

A short to medium annual or biennial with a basal rosette of pinnately lobed leaves, and usually no stem leaves. The pods are longer than their stalks and held at an angle to the main stem.

Found on waste land, on roadsides, in gardens and on sand dunes, this plant flowers from October to May.

Another name for wall rocket is 'stinkweed', because it gives off a smell like that of hydrogen sulphide (rotten eggs) when bruised. Sand rocket (*D. tenuifolia*) is a medium to tall perennial occurring in parts of the South Island. The base of the stem is woody, and there is no rosette. The stem leaves are cut into pinnate lobes. It has yellow petals, with flowers 15–30mm in diameter, and the pods are erect, parallel to the stem.

Hesperis matrionalis *
Dame's violet

Brassicaceae (Mustard Family)
♥ 15–20mm

A medium to tall perennial with simple toothed leaves. Its flowers are white or violet, and are strongly fragrant. The pods are curved upward and up to 100mm long.

It lives on waste land and is also found in old gardens. Flowers from November to April.

The fragrance is stronger at night, which may be related to the fact that the flowers are pollinated by night-flying moths. This species was brought to England from Europe in the 16th century. Its name in French was *violette de Damas*, meaning 'violet from Damascus'. This was misunderstood as *violette des dames*, which, when translated into English, became 'dame's violet'.

Lunaria annua*
Honesty

Brassicaceae (Mustard Family)
15–20mm

A tall biennial plant with branching, hairy stems. The leaves are heart-shaped, dark green, and with coarsely toothed edges. The large elliptical silicules, papery and white-translucent when mature, make this plant easy to recognise.

Honesty lives in waste areas around gardens. It flowers in October and November.

The name *Lunaria* comes from the moon-like appearance of the ripe silicules. Honesty and dame's violet are examples of the many members of this family cultivated for their colourful flowers or pleasant fragrance. Other popular garden plants in this family include wallflower (*Chieranthus*), stock (*Matthiola*), candytuft (*Iberis*), aubretia and alyssum.

Raphanus raphanistrum subsp. *maritimus**
Sea radish

Brassicaceae (Mustard Family)
25–30mm

A medium perennial, with pinnately lobed lower leaves, the terminal lobe being narrower than the four to eight pairs of closely-set lateral leaflets. The upper leaves are simple and spear-shaped, sometimes with a pair of lobes at the base. The plant is rough to the touch, with stiff hairs. The petals are yellow or white, with branching purple veins. The pod narrows to a point at the far end and is strongly constricted into two to six segments, each containing one rounded seed.

It grows on roadsides and on waste land near the coast, flowering from December to March.

Wild radish, *R. raphanistrum* subsp. *raphanistrum**, grows further inland, flowering from October to April. Its pinnate lower leaves have one to four pairs of lateral leaflets, more widely spaced, and the terminal leaflet is the widest. The flowers are yellow, lilac, or white, with purple veins. The pod has five to eight segments with a longer, narrower region between them, and tapers more gradually.

**Pods of sea radish
(actual size)**

Subspecies *maritimus*   Subspecies *raphanistrum*

Rorippa nasturtium-aquaticum*
Watercress

Brassicaceae (Mustard Family)
✔ 2mm

A short to medium, creeping perennial with pinnate leaves. The stem is hollow and juicy, up to 1m long, often with small roots growing from the axils of the leaves. The flowers are in a tight cluster at the stem tips, with pods spreading sideways below. The pods are 2–2.5mm wide, their stalks are 12–15mm long, and they contain two rows of seeds.

Watercress grows in streams, drains and ditches, and is most common in the North Island. It flowers from November to February.

This plant is rich in vitamin C. One-rowed watercress, *R. microphylla**, is a trailing plant with stems up to 1m long. It has larger flowers, pods about 1.5mm wide, stalks 12–20mm long. They contain only one row of seeds. Old leaves turn purplish brown. Commoner in the South Island, it flowers from November to April. Creeping yellowcress, *R. sylvestris**, is found growing in damp places, especially around cultivated areas. Plants are up to 70cm tall, with yellow petals 4–5mm long.

Sisymbrium officinale*
Hedge mustard

Brassicaceae (Mustard Family)
3mm

A medium to tall, erect, hairy annual with a basal rosette of pinnately lobed leaves. The stem is stiff and branches freely. The stem leaves may be pinnate, with spreading, backwardly pointing lobes, or arrow-shaped, with a pair of pointed lobes at the base. The cluster of flowers at the apex of each branch is inconspicuous. The stem of mature plants bears numerous pods on short stalks which are 10–15mm long, erect, and pressed very close to the stem — a distinctive feature. The pods have three ribs on each side.

It is found on roadsides and in waste places, flowering from October to January.

Oriental mustard, *S. orientale**, has flowers 7mm in diameter. Its upper leaves are not pinnate. It has very long (40–100mm) pods spreading widely from the stem.

Small, inconspicuous flowers

Some plants with inconspicuous flowers are included in other groups: see *Galium* sp. (p. 55), *Rorippa nasturtium-aquaticum* and *Sisymbrium officinale* (p.30).

Amaranthus powellii * Amaranthaceae (Amaranth Family)
Redroot 2–3mm

A low to medium, hairy, annual herb, with angular stems, often red. Flowers with four or five green tepals, unequal in length, tapering to a sharply pointed tip. The inflorescence has a main spike up to 250mm long, with a few leaves toward the lower end. There are also a few shorter spikes in the axils of the upper leaves, as seen in the photograph. It is often confused with another redroot, *A. retroflexus**, the tepals of which have square-cut or rounded tips, and which has shorter spikes branching from the main stem.

Redroot lives in and around towns, flowering from December to February.

Prostrate amaranth, *A. deflexus*, is a low mat-forming herb, with dark green leaves, flowers with only two to three tepals, and a dense spike of greenish or pinkish flowers.

Atriplex prostrata * Chenopodiaceae (Goosefoot Family)
Orache 0.5–0.8mm long

A low, spreading annual, branching profusely, with ribbed stems up to 500mm long. Leaves and stems have a slightly mealy appearance, characteristic of this family. The middle and lower leaves vary, but are mostly arrow-shaped, with the leaf base more or less square-cut. Leaf stalks are up to 30mm long.

Found in coastal areas, growing in hollows in sand dunes, on mud flats, and on banks of tidal streams. Like other members of this family it shows adaptations to dry conditions, often in areas where the soil water is excessively salty.

Another common orache is *A. patula**, which has narrower, lance-shaped middle and lower leaves, with leaf stalks up to 15mm long.

31

Chenopodium album*
Fathen

Chenopodiaceae (Goosefoot Family)
✔ 2mm

A medium to tall annual with lance-shaped or rhomboid leaves, sometimes with serrated edges. The plant is dark green, but the mealy covering makes it bluish green, especially in the younger parts. The inflorescence is mealy white, and the leaf shape is very variable.

It is common in inhabited and cultivated areas, flowering from December to May.

The success of this weed is due to its seeds remaining buried in the soil for a long time, and able to germinate when conditions are right. Seeds found buried at an archaeological site known to be 1700 years old were still able to germinate. This plant was one of the earliest food crops, and in Neolithic times and in the Bronze and Iron Ages, its seeds were ground to make flour for bread and gruel. The name *Chenopodium* means 'goose-foot' and refers to the shape of the leaf. The Goosefoot Family includes *Beta maritima,* which has been bred to produce a number of varieties of economic importance: beetroot, sugar beet, mangold and spinach beet. Spinach (*Spinachia oleraceae*) also belongs to this family.

Chenopodium murale*
Nettle-leaved fathen

Chenopodiaceae (Goosefoot Family)
2mm

A medium to tall, mealy, erect, perennial plant, sometimes with a reddish tinge. The leaves are either green on both surfaces or purple on both surfaces. The inflorescence is green or reddish purple.

It grows in waste areas, on cultivated land and on roadsides and flowers from December to May.

A similar plant is jagged fathen (*C. erosum**), a spreading, annual plant with leaves that are often dark purple below (but rarely above). Its inflorescences are often dark red. Clammy goosefoot (*C. pumilio**) is a short to medium spreading annual with relatively smaller, more deeply cut leaves. It has glandular scales which emit an aromatic smell and it has no mealy covering. The leaves are sometimes purple on the under-surface.

*Euphorbia helioscopia**
Sun spurge

Euphorbiaceae (Spurge Family)
✗ 1.5mm

A medium, erect annual with oval leaves that are finely toothed except near the base. The flowers have no petals and no sepals. The inflorescence in this genus consists of a hollow, cup-like structure in which the male flowers are hidden, each consisting of one stamen. The female flower (consisting of a green ovary and style) is on a stalk projecting out of the cup. In this species the inflorescences are in five-rayed umbels (sometimes only three or four rays). On the margins of the cup are three oval, stalked green glands. The stem exudes milky latex when broken.

A common weed of gardens and waste places flowering all the year round.

The plant is poisonous. The genus *Euphorbia* has a wide variety of forms shown by its species, which vary from the small and delicate garden weed, *E. peplus*, described below, to medium-sized and large cactus-like shrubs. The genus also includes the well-known 'Christmas plant', *E. pulcherrima*, also known as poinsettia, which is grown as a pot-plant because of its large scarlet bracts.

*Euphorbia peplus**
Milkweed, Petty spurge

Euphorbiaceae (Spurge Family)
✗ 1.5mm

A low to short annual with oval, entire leaves. The flowers have no petals or sepals. The inflorescence is as described for sun spurge except that the three glands are crescent-shaped, with the points directed outwards. The inflorescences are in three-rayed umbels. The stem exudes milky latex when broken.

This is a very common weed of gardens, waste places and on sandy or shingly areas. It also flowers all the year round.

This plant is poisonous, but several members of this family are important food plants, none more so than the locust-resistant cassava (or manioc) from which comes tapioca. The most economically important member of this family is *Hevea braziliensis*, the rubber tree, tapped for its latex which is cured to make rubber.

Gnaphalium coarctatum *
Purple cudweed

Asteraceae (Daisy Family)
1mm long

A short to tall annual or biennial, often with a single, unbranched stem. If the stem branches, it does so only near the base. The leaves are distinctive in having a dense, *purplish white*, woolly covering on the underside. The upper surface of all except the youngest leaves is hairless, shiny, and *dark green*. The inflorescence is a miniature spike of clusters of tiny flower-heads, with strap-shaped leaves between them.

A common weed of waste areas, lawns, pasture and cultivated land generally. It flowers from September to March.

Creeping cudweed (*G. involucratum*), which is a perennial, has leaves with a dense, *white*, woolly covering on the underside while the upper surface is hairless, shiny and *dark green*. The inflorescence is a small dense cluster of about 10–15 flower-heads, surrounded by a rosette of leaves of different lengths (between one and four times the diameter of a cluster).

Haloragis erecta
Raspweed

Haloragaceae (Raspweed Family)
2mm

A medium to tall, perennial plant with stems square in section and opposite, stalked leaves. The leaves are simple with a deeply toothed margin. The small reddish flowers occur in clusters of three to seven. The flowers have eight stamens.

Raspweed grows along roadsides and on waste areas, flowering from December to February.

The plant in the photograph belongs to the common subspecies *erecta*. The other subspecies *cartilaginea* has more rounded, thicker leaves, and a relatively shorter leaf-stalk. Several members of this family are aquatic, including water milfoil (*Myriophyllum* sp.), frequently grown in aquaria and ornamental garden pools.

Phytolacca octandra *
Inkweed

Phytolaccaceae (Inkweed Family)
✘ 5–7mm

A medium to tall, perennial plant, becoming woody when mature. The leaves are alternate, elliptical, entire, with a pointed tip. The stems and the lower surfaces of the leaf are scattered with white crystalline clusters. The stems are often reddish. Although the flowers are not small their whitish colouring makes them inconspicuous. They have eight stamens (the reason for the name *octandra*). They fruit quickly, so that the inflorescence is generally seen as a tall, narrow raceme of rounded, shiny green fruits, becoming purplish black on ripening, and surrounded by five tepals which turn pink or bright red at that time. The fruits are grooved, showing that they are composed of eight fused carpels.

Inkweed thrives on waste land and cleared ground and flowers from November to August. The plant is poisonous owing to the calcium oxalate crystals on its stems and leaves.

Plantago major *
Broad-leaved plantain

Plantaginaceae (Plantain Family)
4mm

A low to tall, perennial plant with a basal rosette of broad oval leaves, each with five to seven prominent parallel veins. The leaf stalk is slightly winged and may be almost as long as the leaf blade. The spike is greenish and elongated, being 15–300mm long — as long or longer than its stalk. Anthers are pale purple when they first open, later turning brown. They are mounted on the ends of long filaments that project conspicuously from the inflorescence. The anthers produce large amounts of dry, dusty pollen.

It lives is a wide variety of open disturbed areas, particularly damp areas. Flowers from July to April.

Its relative the narrow-leaved plantain or ribwort (*P. lanceolata*) has narrow lance-shaped leaves tapering more gradually to the base. The spike is blackish and oval, about 20–60mm long at the end of a distinctly grooved stalk. Anthers are creamy white when they open, later turning brown.

35

Polygonum aviculare*
Makakaka, Wireweed, Knotgrass

Polygonaceae (Dock Family)
2–3mm

A low, hairless, mat-forming annual, with wiry 'jointed' stems widely spreading close to the ground. It has lance-shaped leaves, those on the young and main stems being larger than those on the branches. There are clusters of one to six flowers in the axils of the leaves, and the flowers are green or white with reddish borders. There is a sheath (an *ochrea*) at the base of each leaf stalk, and the stalk is swollen at the joint — two characteristics of this family. In this species the ochreae are silvery, with jagged edges and a few veins.

It is very common on waste and cultivated ground, flowering from November to June.

Further notes on this plant appear on p. 38.

Polygonum hydropiper*
Water pepper

Polygonaceae (Dock Family)
2.5–3mm

A medium to tall, erect, hairless annual. Its leaves taste strongly peppery and have small translucent spots on them. The leaves are 10–120mm long and 3–20mm wide. Ochreae (see above) are up to 20mm long, reddish brown, possibly with a fringe of a few bristles. The inflorescence of the water pepper is a narrow raceme, which partly curls downward, with flowers well spaced out. Flower stalks are short, hidden inside the bracts until the fruits start maturing.

Water pepper grows in damp areas, beside streams, ponds and lakes, and on poorly drained land. It flowers from November to June.

Hybrids occur between this species and willow weed. A plant of similar appearance is *P. punctatum**; the leaves of which are larger (40–150mm long, 10–40mm wide) and have a slight peppery taste. Its ochreae have a fringe of bristles. The flowers are white or pale green, with flower-stalks usually longer than the bracts. The name *Polygonum* means 'many knees', referring to the jointed appearance of the stem.

*Polygonum persicaria**
Willow weed

Polygonaceae (Dock Family)
2–3mm

A medium, spreading annual with lance-shaped leaves, usually with black areas and spots on the upper surface. The inflorescence is an erect, dense spike of pink flowers, less than 40mm long. Ochreae (p. 36) are green or pink, with a fringe of hairs.

It grows on waste and cultivated land, near to habitation, and flowers all the year round.

Hybrids occur between this species and water pepper. According to folklore, the dark spots on the leaves show where the Devil pinched them on discovering that they lack the hot peppery taste of the leaves of water pepper. Shetland Islanders use this plant as a source of a yellow dye.

Another common species is *P. polystachum**, Indian knotweed, a tall perennial with stout stems, red main veins and pinkish side veins on the leaves, and a copiously branching inflorescence of white flowers on thin red branches. *P. strigosum*, found in northern areas of the North Island, has sparse inflorescences of small pink flowers; its bristly hairiness and arrow-shaped leaves distinguish it from other species.

*Rumex acetosella**
Sheep's sorrel

Polygonaceae (Dock Family)
♥ 2mm

A low to short, hairless, reddish perennial with leaves arrow-shaped or very narrow, with two spreading or forward-pointing lobes at the base. The leaves have a bitter taste. The inflorescence is a narrow raceme of reddish or yellowish flowers.

Sheep's sorrel is abundant on open waste land from sea level to 1500m, particularly in poor, dry habitats. It flowers throughout the year.

The name 'sorrel' is derived from the French word *surele*, meaning 'sour'. It can be used as a pot herb.

37

Rumex crispus*
Curled dock

Polygonaceae (Dock Family)
2mm

A medium to tall perennial with broad, stalked leaves with finely wavy edges. The inflorescence consists of whorls of green flowers, the whorls being very close together, almost touching.

It lives in damp areas such as pastures, beside lakes, streams and ditches, in swamps, and occasionally on drier sites too. Curled dock flowers from November to April.

Clustered dock (*R. conglomeratus**) has similar leaves, though they are not as large. The whorls of green flowers in the inflorescence are spaced apart from each other.

Rumex sagittatus*
Climbing dock

Polygonaceae (Dock Family)
2mm

A climbing or scrambling perennial with stems up to 3m long. The leaves are triangular or spear-shaped. The photograph was taken at the fruiting stage, when the plant is most noticeable, being covered by conspicuous yellow, pink or bright red fruits.

It lives in coastal areas, on waste land and banks, often climbing on hedges, and in gardens. It flowers from November to March.

Notes on Polygonum aviculare (p. 36)
In China and Japan this plant was used as a source of a blue dye, similar to indigo. The stems contain large quantities of silica crystals, making the plant a useful scouring-pad for dishes. A more bizarre use of the plant in the Middle Ages was to stunt the growth of children so that they could become dwarfs in circuses. This was known to William Shakespeare who, in *A Midsummer Night's Dream*, wrote:

> *Get you gone, you dwarf,*
> *You minimus of hindering knotgrass made;*
> *You bead! You acorn!*

In small-leaved wireweed (*P. arenastrum**) the leaves on the young and main stems are about the same length as, or only slightly longer than the leaves on the branches.

Sarcocornia quinqueflora
Glasswort

Chenopodiaceae (Goosefoot Family)
less than 1mm

A low to medium, shrubby perennial with succulent, opposite, scale-like leaves closely pressed to the stem and fused so as to surround it completely. This gives its branches a characteristic 'jointed' appearance. The leaves are translucent and green or reddish, but are often encrusted with mud or salt. The minute flowers are in short-branched, 'jointed' spikes.

It is common on salt marshes and shingly beaches, where it is completely covered at high spring tides. It flowers from November to March.

Senecio bipinnatisectus*
Australian fireweed

Asteraceae (Daisy Family)
2mm

A tall annual (sometimes living for several years) with stem leaves very deeply and pinnately cut into narrow segments. The segments are toothed or sometimes pinnately lobed again, as seen in the photograph. The stem is usually hairless, but may have just a few hairs. The flower-heads have three to four supplementary bracts (see p.116) 1–3mm long, and a single row of 8–13 narrow, inner bracts, 5–7mm long. The small flower-heads have no rays and the disc flowers are greenish yellow.

Common in the North Island in waste areas, coastal areas, pasture, forest margins and clearings. It flowers from December to June.

Another introduced fireweed, *S. diaschides*, is common in Northland. Its leaves are very narrow, the margins with shallow, widely spaced teeth. The leaf-bases of the lower and mid-stem leaves are often deeply cut into three parts, and clasp the stem. Flower-heads have four to six supplementary bracts 1–2mm long and a single row of 8–12 inner bracts, 4.5–5.5mm long. Its disc flowers are yellow.

Senecio glomeratus
Fireweed

Asteraceae (Daisy Family)
2–3mm

A medium annual (which sometimes lives for a few years), with pinnately cut leaves (not as deeply cut as *B. bipinnatisectus*, nor are the segments pinnately cut again). The lobes have a few coarse teeth. The leaves and stems are greyish, with a dense white felt on the underside of the leaves. There are 8–14 supplementary bracts (see p. 116) 1–2.5mm long, and 13 inner bracts, 4.5–6mm long. There are no ray flowers and the disc flowers are yellow.

This plant is very common in a wide range of habitats, from sea level to 1000m. It flowers from November to March.

The leaves of another native fireweed, the cotton fireweed (*S. quadridentatus*) are very narrow and parallel-sided, with entire margins, possibly having a few widely-spaced small teeth. The leaves and stems are greyish with a dense white felt on the undersides of the leaves. There are three to five supplementary bracts 1–1.5 mm long, and 12–13 inner bracts, 6–9mm long.

Regular-shaped flowers

Acaena agnipila*
Bidibidi

Rosaceae (Rose Family)
3–5mm

A short to tall, erect perennial, with pinnate leaves, 80–150mm long. There are 8–13 pairs of toothed leaflets. The inflorescence is a narrow spike of flowers, irregularly scattered towards the base. The flowers have five green sepals but no petals. The mature calyx tube (see below) has 12–55 red spines, 1–2mm long, with barbed tips. *A. agnipila** differs from other members of the genus in being erect rather than prostrate, and having a narrow spike instead of a rounded inflorescence.

Bidibidi lives in dry grassland and waste areas, flowering from October to March.

In *Acaena* the bases of the sepals unite to form a calyx tube, partly surrounding the carpels. When the carpels mature, prominent spines, often with barbed tips, develop on the outside of the calyx tube. These spines aid dispersal of the fruits in the coats of furry animals.

Acaena anserinifolia
Piripiri, Bidibidi

Rosaceae (Rose Family)
✔ 1mm

A prostrate, hairy perennial with pinnate leaves 10–75mm long. There are four to six pairs of toothed leaflets; the end leaflet is longer than it is wide. The inflorescence is a globular cluster of 50–60 flowers, which have four green sepals but no petals. The two stamens with white anthers and the white style give the inflorescence an overall whitish appearance. The mature calyx tube develops four pale brown spines 4–9mm long, with barbed tips, radiating from the inflorescence.

This bidibidi is found along forest margins and in shrubland from lowland to high alpine regions. It flowers from December to April

The leaves may be used as tea. This species is unusual in that it has become naturalised in Britain, by way of Australia, carried as fruits entangled in raw wool.

41

Allium triquetrum*
Three-cornered garlic

Alliaceae (Onion Family)
15mm

A medium perennial, growing from bulbs. The plant has an unpleasant, garlic-like smell. The leaves are long, narrow and solid, and are easily crushed, producing strong-smelling juice. They arise from the base of the plant, sheathing the inflorescence stalk. The name 'three-cornered' comes from this stalk which is triangular in section, with a pronounced 'wing' at each corner. The inflorescence is a dense cluster of about 3–15 white flowers on short stalks. As the flowers open, these stalks lengthen and the flowers droop. The inner surface of each tepal has a central green stripe.

A common weed, found in gardens and waste places. It flowers in October and November.

It is probably an escape from kitchen gardens. Many members of the Onion Family (onion, shallot, garlic, leek, chive) are cultivated for their flavour and some for food too. A few are well known as ornamental plants, including agapanthus. *A. triquetrum* may be confused with the wild onion, *A. vineale**, but this has hollow leaves, roughly circular in section, as is the inflorescence stalk. Wild onion usually produces small bulbs (*bulbils*) instead of flowers.

Anagallis arvensis*
Scarlet pimpernel

Primulaceae (Primrose Family)
8mm

A low-growing annual with square stems. The leaves are without stalks and have black dots (glands) on the underside. The brick-red, star-like flowers, with the sepals clearly visible between the petals, distinguish this species from all others. The petals may be toothed at the tip and have red or black hairs on their margins.

Scarlet pimpernel is very common and widespread on open waste and cultivated land, and flowers all the year round.

This is sometimes known as the 'poor man's weather-glass', as the flowers are said to close just before it rains. The plant shown in the photograph belongs to the common subspecies *arvensis*, and to the red-flowered variety *arvensis*, so the full name of this small plant is *Anagallis arvensis* subsp. *arvensis* var. *arvensis*.

Aptenia cordifolia*
Aptenia

Aizoaceae (Mesembryanthemum Family)
20–25mm

A low, spreading, perennial herb with stems up to 300mm or more long. The leaves are fleshy but flat (not swollen or rounded in section), and they are oval to triangular in shape. The tiny swellings on the leaf, as seen on the leaf at the bottom centre of the photograph, are clear but not glittering. They also occur on the sepals. The four sepals, all larger than the petals, confirm the identity of this species.

It grows in rocky or sandy areas on the coast, and flowers all the year round.

The genus name *Aptenia* means 'without wings', referring to the lack of wings on the fruit that occur in some other genera of this family. The heart-shaped leaves give it the species name *cordifolia*.

Borago officinalis*
Borage

Boraginaceae (Borage Family)
✔ 20–25mm

A short to medium annual or biennial. The plant is bristly-hairy with wavy-edged leaves. The flowers are closely clustered and are distinguished by the purplish black stamens projecting from the centre of each flower.

Found on roadsides and waste land, usually as a garden escape. It flowers from September to May.

Borage can be used as a salad, in soups, or cooked and eaten like spinach. The flowers may be floated in cocktails to garnish them. The name *Borago* comes from the Latin *burra*, a shaggy garment, referring to the plant's dense covering of bristly hairs. This is a feature of most members of the Borage Family. The inflorescence is typically coiled, an example being water forget-me-not (p. 64). The petals are usually fused into a tube, which may end in five shallow lobes or in a flattened disc of five rounded lobes. A feature of this family is that there is often a coloured scale on each petal at the 'throat' of the flower. Several of the Borage Family are grown as ornamental plants, including heliotrope (*Heliotropium*), forget-me-not (including Chatham Island forget-me-not), viper's bugloss, alkanet (*Anchusa*), lungwort (*Pulmonaria*), borage and comfrey.

Calandrinia menziesii *
Curnow's curse

Portulacaceae (Purslane Family)
18–20mm

A short to medium annual, with a basal rosette of oval to spoon-shaped leaves, sheathing the stem. Stem leaves and bracts are similar, with stalks. The two sepals are spear-shaped, large (about 7mm x 5mm) and free at the base. Stigmas are white.

It is found on waste and cultivated land, flowering from October to December.

C. compressa has similar showy purple flowers, that are slightly smaller. The stem leaves and bracts have no stalks. The two sepals are joined together at the base. Stigmas are purple. Some species of *Calandrinia* are grown as ornamental garden plants.

Calystegia sepium *
Akapohue, Nahinahi, Panake, Pink bindweed

Convolvulaceae (Bindweed Family)
➕ *m* 40-60mm

A climbing perennial with distinctly triangular or arrow-shaped leaves. The five sepals are enclosed by two large bracts that do not overlap each other. Petals are pink with a white band down the centre, or occasionally all white. The style is longer than the stamens.

It is common on roadsides, waste areas, swamps and forest margins. It flowers from September to February.

The name *Calystegia* comes from the Greek *kalyx stegon*, meaning 'calyx cover' which refers to the two large bracts covering the calyx. The roots and shoots were cooked and eaten by the Maori, but in some parts of the world the plant is regarded as a purgative, possibly because of differences between varieties. It is advisable not to use this plant for food.

Great bindweed (*C. silvatica* *) has larger (60–75mm diameter) white flowers (rarely pink). The bracts which enclose the sepals overlap each other. This and the fact that the styles are equal to, or only slightly longer than, the stamens make it easy to tell this plant from *C. sepium*. The flowers of panahi or shore bindweed (*C. soldanella*) are only 30–35mm in diameter. They are pink, and each petal has a central white stripe. The leaves are fleshy and kidney-shaped. It is common in coastal areas, growing on sand.

Carduus tenuiflorus*
Winged thistle

Asteraceae (Daisy Family)
7–15mm

A short to tall annual or biennial covered with cobweb-like white hairs. The stems have thorny wings and the leaves are densely white-haired beneath. The leaves are spiny. The flower-heads are smaller and paler than those of most thistles. They have no stalks and are grouped in clusters of up to 8 at the ends of the stems.

This plant grows in waste areas, on sand dunes, beside roads, and in pasture and tussock grassland. It flowers in November and December.

Slender winged thistle (*C. pycnocephalus**) is similar in appearance, but has narrower stem wings (only 2mm wide) between clusters of spines, compared with wings 2–3mm wide or even up to 10mm wide in *C. tenuiflorus*. Its flower heads are shortly stalked in clusters that are not so compact as those of *C. tenuiflorus*.

Carpobrotus edulis*
Ice plant, Cape fig, Hottentot fig

Aizoaceae (Mesembryanthemum Family)
✔ 80–100mm

A short, spreading perennial with long, woody stems, up to 6m long. The leaves are thick and fleshy, sharply triangular in section, and have a bitter taste. The yellow petals fade to a pinkish orange colour. At first glance this might be taken for one of the Daisy Family but, although the flowers have many petals and stamens, their structure is otherwise that of a normal flower.

It is found on the coast, growing on cliffs and sand dunes. It flowers from October to February.

The inner parts of the fruit may be eaten, giving the plant its scientific name *Carpobrotus*, which comes from the Greek and means 'fruit edible'. The leaves too, are edible, usually being pickled first to preserve them. The thick fleshy leaves, consisting mainly of special water-storage tissues, are typical of plants that live in very dry places. This plant has also been known as *Mesembryanthemum*, from which is derived one of its common names, 'Sally-my-handsome', in Cornwall, England.

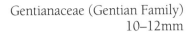

Centaurium erythraea*
Centaury

Gentianaceae (Gentian Family)
10–12mm

A low to short, hairless annual or biennial, growing from a basal rosette, with a few narrow three-veined leaves on the stems. The bracts of the inflorescence are longer than the sepals. Flowers are almost unstalked, in dense clusters. They have five partly fused sepals, ending in narrow tips,
It is a very common plant of open habitats from lowland to 700m. It flowers from November to April.
A plant of similar appearance is *C. tenuiflorum**, but this does not have a well defined basal rosette at flowering time. Its flowers are shortly stalked, smaller than those of *C. erythraea*, and with narrow, more sharply pointed corolla lobes.

Cerastium fontanum*
Mouse-ear chickweed

Caryophyllaceae (Pink Family)
6–7mm

A low to short perennial, often creeping, though sometimes erect. As well as branches ending in an inflorescence, there are leafy, non-flowering branches. The petals are notched at the tip, but not for more than one-third of their length. The petals equal the sepals in length. The sepals have non-glandular hairs (ending in a fine point, not a rounded 'knob'). The tips of the hairs do not project beyond the tips of the sepals. It lives in grassy places, on roadsides and in waste areas, scrub, sand dunes and the banks of streams. It flowers from November to April.

There are several common species in this genus. Snow-in-summer (*C. tomentosum**) is covered with silvery, felted hairs. Its petals are about twice as long as the sepals, as they are also in field chickweed (*C. arvense**). The latter occurs only in the South Island, lacks the silvery felting and has short glandular hairs on its sepals. All other species have petals about as long as the sepals. Annual mouse-ear chickweed (*C. glomeratum**) has both glandular and non-glandular hairs on its sepals. The non-glandular hairs are long, and some project beyond the tips of the sepals. In little mouse-ear chickweed (*C. semidecandrum**), the non-glandular hairs do not project beyond the sepal tips.

46

Cirsium arvense*
Californian thistle

Asteraceae (Daisy Family)
25–30mm

A medium to tall perennial growing from a rhizome. It has spiny leaves but no spines on the stem or bracts. The flower-heads consist only of tubular flowers and are shortly stalked, in clusters, with purplish bracts. There is no latex.

It grows in waste places, on roadsides and in cultivated land. It is often found in dry areas, such as sand dunes, screes and stony ground. It flowers from December to February.

Scotch thistle (*C. vulgare**) grows from a tap root. It has long, sharp, pale spines on the leaves, the winged stems and the bracts. The narrow wings arise from the bases of the leaves and run down the stems. The undersides of the leaves are covered with dense grey hairs. The flower-heads are large (25-50mm diameter) and are solitary or in clusters of two or three. Although *C. vulgare* is known as scotch thistle, the Scottish national emblem is the cotton thistle (*Onopordum acanthium**). This grows from a tap root and has sharp spines on its leaves, broadly winged stems and bracts. The bracts are covered with cottony hairs, and end in the long, yellowish spines. The flower-head has the sharply 'waisted' shape of the heraldic emblem, which distinguishes it from *Carduus* and *Cirsium*.

Clematis paniculata
Puawhananga, Pikiarero

Ranunculaceae (Buttercup Family)
50–60mm

A tall, woody, climbing perennial with opposite leaves (not alternate, as in most members of this family) consisting of three leaflets. The flowers on a plant are either all male or all female. They are in clusters of six or more, each usually with six white, petal-like sepals. The number of sepals may vary between five and eight. There are no petals. Male flowers have over 50 stamens, with mauve anthers. Female flowers are slightly smaller, with a few infertile stamens and numerous carpels.

C. paniculata lives in lowland and low montane forest, more commonly around the margins. It flowers from August to November.

47

*Clematis vitalba**
Old man's beard, Traveller's joy

Ranunculaceae (Buttercup Family)
16–20mm

A tall, woody, climbing perennial with opposite, pinnate leaves, usually with five leaflets. The leaf and leaflet stalks twine around supports. Flowers occur in the leaf axils and at the ends of the stem. The flowers have four or five petal-like sepals, but no petals. The sepals are white inside; outside they are greenish cream, with a white border. The flowers have a pleasant smell and possess both male and female parts. The fruits of this species give it one of its names, as each has a long, persistent style, covered with long greyish hairs.

It lives in scrub, hedges, and forest margins, flowering from March to October.

Old man's beard has become an annoying weed where it grows in damaged native forest. Many people call this plant by its scientific name, *clematis,* instead of using its common names. But there are frequent disagreements as to how the name should be pronounced: whether it is 'clematis' (short 'e'), 'cleematis' (long 'e'), or 'claymatis' is a matter of opinion. The first is suitable for gardeners' chat, though either one of the other pronunciations is more correct for scientific use. Whatever version is used, the accent is on the first syllable, not the second.

*Crocosmia x crocosmiiflora**
Montbretia

Iridaceae (Iris Family)
40–50mm

A medium to tall, hairless plant, forming dense clumps. The leaves are flat. The inflorescence is 150–300mm long, consisting of a one-sided spike, slightly branched or unbranched, with a zig-zag stalk. Flowers are tubular at the base, with six lobes equal in length. The three branches of the style are three-lobed at their tips.

Crocosmia x crocosmiiflora is found on roadsides, grassy areas and waste land, abundant in places. Flowers from December to February.

The 'x' in the name of this plant indicates that it is a hybrid. A related species is *C. paniculata**, found in Nelson and Westland; this is identified by its folded or pleated leaves, its branched inflorescence and its smaller (15mm) orange flowers, tinged with crimson.

Datura stramonium*
Thorn apple

Solanaceae (Nightshade Family)
✚ ✗ 60–80mm long

A medium to tall annual with an unpleasant smell. The leaves are oval, with large teeth. The flowers are erect and open in the evenings, except in rainy weather. The fruits are green, oval, about 20mm in diameter and covered with long, green thorns.

It lives in waste areas and on roadsides and flowers from November to April.

Thorn apple, like several other members of this family, contains the hallucinogenic and very poisonous alkaloid, scopolamine. It is poisonous in large quantities but has medical uses as a hypnotic when taken in small, carefully prescribed doses. It is said that the seeds of thorn apple were used at the temple of Apollo, in ancient Greece, to make the priests of the Oracle issue wild and frenzied proclamations, supposedly to have come from the gods.

Dianella nigra
Turutu, Blueberry, Ink-berry

Phormiaceae (Harakeke Family)
8mm

A medium, perennial plant with fans of long, narrow, glossy leaves arising from short, woody shoots. The leaves are edged dark reddish brown at the base, and they are strongly keeled and folded. Just above the region where it sheaths a younger leaf, the two sides of the leaf are pressed tightly together, almost becoming fused. Above, the leaf opens out to become almost flat, though still with a noticeable keel. The inflorescence is a much-branched wiry stalk bearing small, greenish white flowers and greenish, oval, fleshy fruits. The six tepals are alike in colour and size, the inner three being slightly wider than the outer three. The six stamens are distinctive, having swollen, yellow filaments, as seen in the photograph. Later, the fruits ripen to develop a greyish white to strong blue colour.

It is found on banks and on banked roadsides, often in shady places, and on the forest floor, especially at the edges of tracks. It flowers in November and December.

*Dianthus armeria**
Deptford pink

Caryophyllaceae (Pink Family)
8–15mm

A medium, hairless or softly hairy annual or biennial, dark green in colour (in contrast to the greyish green of many other pinks), with intensely pinkish red flowers. The flowers are in dense clusters of 2–10, closely surrounded by long, leaf-like bracts.

Deptford pink lives in grassy places, roadsides and on sand dunes. It flowers from November to March.

All members of the Pink Family have opposite leaves, and regular flowers with free petals. Another family feature is that the stems are often swollen at the bases of the leaves and branches, giving them a 'jointed' appearance. Branching is often dichotomous, that is, a stem branches into two *equal* branches, which in turn branch into two equal branches, and so on. The family includes a few ornamental and garden plants such as pinks, carnations and sweet-william (which are all species of *Dianthus*), as well as *Lychnis*, *Silene*, and *Gypsophila*.

Disphyma australe
Horokaka, Ngarangara, Maori ice plant

Aizoaceae (Mesembryanthemum Family)
✔ *m* 20–40mm

A short, spreading perennial with thick, fleshy leaves, triangular in section but more rounded than those of *Carpobrotus*. They end in a short, sharp point. The flowers are solitary, with white or pink petals.

Widespread in coastal regions, it flowers from October to January.

The inner part of the fruit and the pickled leaves can be eaten. There is a hybrid genus, known as *Carpophyma*, which is a naturally occurring cross between *Carpobrotus edulis* and *D. australe*. The flowers are of intermediate size (45–60mm in diameter) and are of various colours including pink, yellow, orangy pink, and white. No fruits are formed by this hybrid.

Plants in this family are usually very succulent, with thick, fleshy leaves. These act as water-storage tissues, so allowing the plants to survive long dry periods, or to live in salty habitats where excess salt makes it difficult for the plants to absorb water.

Drosera binata
Sundew

Droseraceae (Sundew Family)
15–20mm

A short to medium plant with very narrow leaves (2mm wide), forked at least once and covered with sticky hairs. Flower-stalks are dark green or black and bear loose clusters of sweet-scented flowers.

Sundew lives in boggy places from lowland up to 300m, flowering from November to February.

The sticky hairs on the leaves gives the plant a dewy appearance. The genus name is derived from the Greek *droseros*, meaning 'dewy'. *D. arcturi* has strap-shaped leaves (about 8mm wide); the flower stalks bear only one flower (rarely two or three). In *D. stenopetala*, the strap-shaped leaves (about 5mm wide) broaden to a spoon-shaped tip, which is edged with prominent, radiating, sticky hairs. The flower-stalks are dark reddish and narrow, bearing a single flower. When a small insect lands on a leaf the long sticky hairs bend over, trapping the insect in the sticky liquid secreted from the swollen end of the hair. The secretion contains substances that digest the soft parts of the insect's body. The digested materials are then absorbed into the leaf and used as food materials by the plant. Afterwards the hairs uncurl and the dry outer parts of the dead insect fall away. Since these plants are insectivorous, they are able to live in boggy soils where other plants find difficulty in absorbing nutrients.

*Duchesnea indica**
Indian strawberry

Rosaceae (Rose Family)
10–12mm

A low to short, mat-forming perennial with strawberry-like trefoil leaves. The solitary flowers look at first glance like buttercups, but the prominent epicalyx, with five leafy segments, confirms its identity. The fruit is red and strawberry-like in appearance but is drier and not really edible.

It is a garden escape which now lives in shady, damp places on forest margins, and in light shade in reserves and waste land. It flowers from July to April.

51

Echium vulgare *
Viper's bugloss

Boraginaceae (Borage Family)
✚ 15–20mm

A short to tall, annual or biennial plant with flowers in a densely branched spike. Stems and leaves are covered with stiff hairs, as is often found in this family (p. 43). The flowers turn from pink to bright blue as they mature. The stamens have long pink filaments and project beyond the tube of the flower.

This is a very common weed of roadsides and waste land. It flowers from November to January.

The fruits consist of four nutlets looking rather like a snake's head. For this reason, it was formerly used as a cure for snake-bite. The related plant, Paterson's curse (*E. plantagineum* *), is common in the North Island, and rare in the South Island. Its flowers are larger, and only two of the stamens project from the tube.

Epilobium billardiereanum
Willowherb

Onagraceae (Willowherb Family)
10–15mm

A tall, erect perennial. Its leaves are narrow, or narrowly oval, toothed, with very short stalks. Flowers may be white or rose-purple; pods are greyish green.

It lives in many habitats from sea level to about 300m. Flowers from December to February.

Tall willowherb (*E. tetragonum*) is common in damp places in the north of the North Island. The leaves are stalkless, their margins running down into raised lines on the stems. Flowers are rose-purple to mauve, from November to January.

The willowherbs

A total of 42 species of willowherb can be found in New Zealand, 37 of them native. Identifying individual willowherb species is difficult, but the *Epilobium* genus has features which make it easy to pick out a willowherb from other types of plant:

- Narrowly oval leaves (reminding us of willow leaves)
- Petals are alike in size and shape and are notched at the tips
- Petals are white or a shade of pink
- The fruit is very long and narrow (from an inferior ovary)
- The wall of the fruit splits into four very narrow segments
- The pod contains numerous seeds, each with a tuft of silky hairs

Erica lusitanica*
Spanish heath

Ericaceae (Heath Family)
3–5mm long

A tall, hairless shrub. Its leaves are narrow, with three to four in a whorl. The flower has four or five free sepals. The corolla of four or five fused petals is narrow and bell-shaped. The lobes of the corolla are very short compared with the tube. The petals are pink in bud, and become white when they open.

It lives on rocky hillsides and banks, scrub and grassland, flowering from March to December.

Small specimens of tree heath (*E. arborea**) may be mistaken for Spanish heath, but a distinguishing feature is that the stigma of Spanish heath is red-tipped, while that of the tree heath is white or light green. Tree heath grows up to 5m high. The heaths are a family of low-growing shrubby plants with leathery, evergreen leaves. The family includes the genus *Vaccinium* which produces blueberries, bilberries and cranberries. Several members of the family are grown as ornamental garden plants, including *Rhododendron*, *Pieris*, *Gaultheria* (p. 55), and many cultivated varieties of heath (*Erica*).

Erodium moschatum*
Musky storksbill

Geraniaceae (Geranium Family)
8–12mm

A low to medium, glandular-hairy plant, sticky to the touch, with a musky smell. The leaves are pinnate, up to 300mm long, with oval, toothed leaflets, rarely pinnately lobed. The inflorescence is an umbel of about 12 flowers. Each flower has 10 stamens in two whorls of five, the inner whorl without anthers. The beak of the fruit is 30–35mm long, covered with very fine, very short hairs.

Found in a variety of open places, including roadsides, lawns and pasture. Flowers from September to November.

Storksbill (*E. cicutarium**) lacks the smell of musky storksbill, is less sticky and its leaves are fern-like. The name 'storksbill' is given to this and similar plants because of the resemblance of the ripening fruit to the head and tapering bill of a stork. A cluster of storksbill fruits can be seen on the left of the photograph.

Eschscholzia californica*
Californian poppy

Papaveraceae (Poppy Family)
30–50mm

A low to medium, hairless annual or perennial with feathery leaves. The sepals are fused to form a pointed hood, which drops off when the flower-bud opens. It has four large, showy yellow or orange petals. The anthers are much longer than the filaments.

This poppy lives in dry places beside roads and on waste land, flowering from October to February.

This plant has fused sepals, but most members of the Poppy Family have separate sepals. Most poppies also have large, showy petals, but do not usually produce nectar — insects visit the flowers to collect the pollen. Many members of this family produce poisonous latex. The opium poppy is the only economically important member of this family, as the drug opium is obtained from its latex. It is not often that a plant causes a war, but this happened in 1839–42, when the so-called Opium War broke out between Britain and China, as a result of disagreements over the trading of opium by Britain. This war led to the ceding of Hong Kong to Britain, due to be returned to China in 1997. The seeds of the opium poppy are used in baking, but are harmless as they do not contain opium. Poppy-seed oil is used in foodstuffs and in paint and soap making.

Fragaria vesca*
Alpine strawberry

Rosaceae (Rose Family)
✔ 12–18mm

A low to short perennial with runners. The leaves are trefoil, bright green, with long, silky hairs on the upper surface. The flowering stems have 3–10 long-stalked flowers. The flower has five triangular sepals, surrounded by an epicalyx of five narrow, entire segments. The fruit is a smaller version of the commercial strawberry.

Alpine strawberry lives in damp areas, on roadsides, waste land, and in clearings in forests, from sea level to 1000m. It flowers from November to April.

*Galium aparine**
Cleavers, Goosegrass

Rubiaceae (Bedstraw Family)
1–1.5mm

A medium to tall, climbing annual with square stems, the angles having stiff, hooked hairs. There are stiff hairs on the leaf margins and on the underside midrib of the leaves, so that the whole plant clings to clothing or animals' fur. The leaves are apparently (see p. 77) in whorls of six to eight, with pointed tips. There are minute flowers in few-flowered clusters, the stalks of the clusters being longer than the leaves. The fruits also bear hooked hairs, which help in their dispersal.

It grows where it can obtain support from other plants, in waste areas, forest margins, under hedges, in weedy gardens and pastures. Goosegrass flowers from July to March.

The plant is called 'goosegrass' because it was at one time fed to newly-hatched goslings. The name 'cleavers' refers to its tendency to cling to (or *cleave* to) passersby. Marsh bedstraw (*G. palustre*) has similar flowers, in clusters of 10 or more. It lacks the hooked hairs but the angles of the stem are rough to the touch.

Gaultheria crassa
Koropuka

Ericaceae (Heath Family)
5mm

A slightly hairy, much-branched shrub, up to 1m tall, though shorter at higher altitudes. Its leaves are alternate, thick, leathery and brownish green, and about 10–15mm long and 5–10mm wide. The flowers are white and waxy, in clusters about 40mm long. The sepals have reddish tips. Fruits are round, dry capsules, brown when ripe, surrounded by a dry calyx.

Widely occurring from 700m to 1700m, it flowers from February to April.

Snowberry (*G. depressa*) is a low-growing shrub with solitary, white flowers. The fruits are red, pink or white fleshy capsules, surrounded by a dry calyx. A similar plant is *Pernettya macrostigma*, a short prostrate shrub, with solitary flowers in the axils of narrow, finely toothed leaves. Its fleshy berries are partly surrounded by a fleshy calyx. Berries and calyx range from white to dark red.

Gentianella bellidifolia
Gentian

Gentianaceae (Gentian Family)
20mm

A short perennial with fleshy, tufted basal leaves, oval to spoon-shaped, 10–15mm long, 5–7mm wide. There are several stems, unbranched or slightly branched, and three to four pairs of smaller stem leaves. The flowers are terminal and solitary or in clusters of up to six. The calyx is about half the length of the corolla; its lobes are at least three times as long as its tube; the notch between the margins of adjacent lobes is narrow, and tapers to a point. The corolla is divided at least three-quarters of the way to the base into bluntly pointed lobes. The fine purple veins on the petals are a distinctive feature.

Gentian lives in tussock grassland and boggy places from 600m to 1800m. It flowers from January to March.

Geranium dissectum*
Cut-leaved cranesbill

Geraniaceae (Geranium Family)
✔ *m* 8–10mm

A short to medium, hairy annual, with the hairs all backwardly pointing. The rounded leaves are cut almost to the base into five to seven narrow segments which may be three-lobed or pinnately lobed. The flowers of cut-leaved cranesbill are usually in twos, the petals notched, with a short claw. The stalk of the inflorescence is shorter than the leaflike bract at its base. The sepals spread out widely and end in a stiff bristle 1mm or more long.

It lives in bare places, especially around buildings, and flowers from November to February.

The roots of this plant are edible. The roots of the related matuakumara (*G. homeanum*), growing as a weed in the kumara beds, were eaten by the Maori when food was scarce. Dovesfoot cranesbill (*G. molle**) also has rounded leaves, but these may have up to nine segments, and are cut only to about three-quarters of the way to the base. The petals are deeply notched, with a very short claw. The sepals end in a sharp tip, not a distinct bristle. Small-flowered cranesbill (*G. pusillum**) has round leaves with five to nine segments.

Geranium microphyllum
Cranesbill

Geraniaceae (Geranium family)
15–20mm

A low, softly hairy perennial, the hairs on the stem backwardly pointing. The leaves are rounded to kidney-shaped in outline, but three- to five-lobed, usually almost to the midrib. The flowers are usually in twos, the petals slightly notched, with a short claw on stems usually 6cm or more long. The sepals spread out widely and end in a short, stiff bristle. There is usually a thin purple line on the margin of each sepal. The beak of the fruit is 7–11mm long.

Cranesbill lives in grassland among tussocks, and in rocky places, from lowland to 1500m. It flowers from October to February.

Most species of *Geranium* have pinkish, mauve or rose flowers but in *G. microphyllum* and *G. sessiliflorum* the flowers are white. The flowers of *G. sessiliflorum* are solitary and have narrower petals and the flowering stems are short, usually less than 3cm long.

Geranium retrorsum
Cranesbill

Geraniaceae (Geranium Family)
6–10mm

A medium perennial with rounded leaves cut almost to the base into lobed segments. The hairs are short and bent near the base, pointing backwards down the stem and leaf-stalks, and are closely pressed to them. The flowers are in twos. The sepals spread widely and have a prominent, stiff bristle about 1mm long.

It lives in grassland and scrub, flowering from October to April.

The cranesbills are given this name because the ripe fruit has the appearance of the head and long bill of a crane, as can be seen on the left of the photograph. The name 'geranium' comes from the Greek, *garanos*', meaning 'crane'. When the fruit is ripe and dry, the carpels split away at the base and curl upward, still attached to the central 'beak'. In some species this happens so violently that the seed is thrown from the plant. In other species the whole carpel wall, and the enclosed seed, splits explosively and travels some distance from the plant.

Geranium robertianum*
Herb Robert

Geraniaceae (Geranium Family)
20mm

A medium annual with leaves of three leaflets, one- or two-pinnately lobed. The stems and leaves are usually tinged with red or are almost entirely red. The plant has a strong and rather unpleasant smell. Flowers are in twos; the petals have three whitish stripes and are very slightly notched at the tips. The limb and claw are equal in length. Sepals are erect and end in a bristle. The pollen is orange.

It is widely distributed on roadsides, in gardens, and in scrub and forest margins, especially in shady locations. It flowers from September to May.

The name 'Robert' is thought by some to have come from the Greek *ruberta*, meaning 'red', and referring to the distinctive red colour of the stem and leaves. But other authorities believe that the plant was named after Robert Duke of Normandy, a famous medical scholar. Another candidate for having the plant named after him is Abbé Robert, who founded the Cistercian Order of monks in the 11th century. Small herb Robert, or little Robin (*G. purpureum**) has reddish stems and leaf-stalks; the leaves too may be reddish. The leaves are divided into five oval lobes which are pinnately lobed. The claw of the petals is slightly longer than the limb; sepals are reddish and upright. The anthers produce yellow pollen.

Hebe lycopodioides
Whipcord hebe

Scrophulariaceae (Foxglove Family)
5–8mm

A tall, branching shrub, with small, closely overlapping leaves, covering the branches to give the characteristic 'whipcord' appearance. Clusters of 3–12 small, white flowers, with four petals and four sepals, appear at the ends of the branches. There are several species of *Hebe* with a similar appearance, but *H. lycopodioides* is the commonest.

It lives in dry tussock and herbfields in the eastern mountains of the South Island, at 900m to 1700m, and flowers in December and January.

The genus *Hebe* is named after Hebe, the Greek goddess of Youth, whose chief task was to hand round nectar and ambrosia to the gods when they were feasting.

Hedychium gardnerianum*
Wild ginger

Zingiberaceae (Ginger Family)
70mm long

A perennial sending up unbranched leafy stems from a fleshy rootstock. The leaves are large and have no leaf-stalk or, at most, a very short one, and are arranged in two rows on opposite sides of the stem. The plant is distinguished from other gingers by the pale lemon flowers with a prominent red filament on the fertile stamen. The other five stamens are infertile and look like petals.

Wild ginger grows on roadsides, and flowers in February and March. It is a troublesome weed.

The other wild ginger frequently found in New Zealand is *H. flavescens**. This has an appearance similar to that of *H. gardnerianum*, but its inflorescence is more cone-shaped, with creamy white, fragrant flowers. Several species of *Hedychium* are cultivated in gardens for ornament and may occasionally escape to the wild. The ginger used as a flavouring, the dead rhizome either whole or ground, comes from *Zingiber officinale*, a native of South-East Asia. Other members of the family produce turmeric and cardamoms.

Hypericum androsaemum*
Tutsan

Clusiaceae (St. John's Wort Family)
✚ 15–25mm

A medium to tall shrub with two wings down opposite sides of the stem. The stems are often reddish in colour. The leaves are oval and give off an aromatic smell when crushed. The petals are about the same length as or a little longer than the sepals. The stamens are many, in bundles of five. There are three styles, which are about half as long as the ovary. The fruit is rounded and fleshy, reddish, becoming black when fully ripe.

Tutsan lives in scrub, in open forest, and in waste areas. It flowers from November to February.

The name comes from the French *toute-sain*, meaning 'all heal'. It has the reputation of healing a variety of conditions, and its leaves were often placed on open wounds.

Hypericum perforatum *
Perforate St. John's wort

Clusiaceae (St. John's Wort Family)
✘ 20mm

A medium, perennial herb, with two narrow ridges down opposite sides of the stem. The leaves have translucent dots, looking like pin-holes. The petals have tiny black dots (glands) on them, particularly on their margins. These may be scattered on the sepals. The leaves have no black glands.

It is very common on roadsides, waste areas, and grassy places. It flowers from December to May.

The common name of this plant comes from the fact that, in Europe, it flowers on or around St. John's Day, 24 June. When crushed, the flowers exude a red sap and this association with blood made the plant an important one in folklore. In many countries it was the custom to hang a sprig of St. John's wort over the door of the house on St. John's Day, to ward off evil spirits. For the same reason it was hung above pictures. This custom gives rise to its scientific name, from the Greek *hyper* (above) and *eikon* (a picture).

Superstition aside, this plant is one of the most toxic pasture weeds in New Zealand.

Libertia peregrinans
Libertia

Iridaceae (Iris Family)
20mm

A medium to tall perennial with green leaves, tending to become copper-coloured where they are exposed to sunlight. The flower buds are brownish and about equal in length to the ovary. All six tepals are white, the inner three being broader than the outer three, and less than twice as long. The inner tepals have a narrow base region so that, from above the flower, almost the whole of each outer tepal can be seen. The anthers are dark orange-brown.

Libertia is locally common in the southern half of the North Island and in many areas of the South Island, flowering from October to January.

The inner tepals of *L. ixioides* (Mikoikoi, tukauki, manga-a-huri papa) are broader and longer than the outer tepals, so that only the tips of the outer tepals can be seen when looking down on the flower. Its anthers are off-white.

Lilium tigrinum*
Tiger lily

Liliaceae (Lily Family)
60–100mm long

A medium to tall perennial, growing from a large whitish or yellowish bulb. The flowering stem bears about five to six large flowers, with the characteristic lily features of long protruding stamen and curved-back tepals. The tepals are bright orange-red in the most commonly found variety, but numerous cultivated varieties, such as the one in the photograph, have become naturalised.

It grows by roadsides and on waste areas, flowering in January and February.

The Iris Family (see *Libertia*) and the Lily Family may be confused because they both have two whorls of three showy tepals. Irises have three stamens; the ovary is inferior and has a three-lobed style, often long and narrow, or broad and petal-like. Members of this family are illustrated on pp. 48, 60, 68, 70 and 76. Lilies have three stamens in two whorls of three and a superior ovary. This family includes many showy cultivated plants such as tulip, crocus, and fritillary.

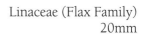

Linum bienne*
Pale flax

Linaceae (Flax Family)
20mm

A short to tall, hairless annual or perennial, with small, narrow leaves alternately arranged on upright, slender stems, which may branch near the base. Petals are 7–11mm long, sepals 4–6mm long.

It grows in waste areas and pastures and flowers from November to April.

Yellow flax (*L. trigynum**) is similar to pale flax but has yellow flowers (12mm). It grows in waste places and sandy areas near the coast, and flowers from September to July.

Linseed (*L. usitatissimum**) has larger flowers (petals 12–18mm long, sepals 6–10mm long) and larger leaves. Its petals may be blue or white. The plant is poisonous. The species name *usitatissimum* means 'most useful' and is well-deserved. The stems are the source of flax fibre, which is made into linen fabric and thread. The seeds are crushed to yield linseed oil, used as a base for paints and for treating timber. At one time it was widely used for making the floor covering linoleum, or 'lino'.

Lythrum hyssopifolia*
Hyssop loosestrife

Lythraceae (Loosestrife Family)
4–6mm

A short to medium annual with pinkish, square stems. Leaves are narrow and alternate, with no stalks or very short stalks. The flowers are small, with six pink, crumpled petals and four to seven stamens of different lengths. The bases of the sepals are fused to make an elongated calyx tube; the stamens are mounted at the lower end of this and the petals are mounted on its rim.

It grows in open damp places and roadsides, and flowers from December to February.

Rose loosestrife (*L. junceum**) has much larger flowers (8–12mm diameter), with six rose-pink, crumpled petals. The calyx tube has small reddish spots half-way along it. It lives on damp ground beside inland waters. Opposite leaves are a feature of most members of the Loosestrife Family, but *Lythrum* has alternate leaves.

Lychnis coronaria*
Rose campion

Caryophyllaceae (Pink Family)
20–30mm

A short to tall perennial with a woolly covering of silvery hairs, giving it an easily recognisable appearance. The leaves are lance-shaped, the blade narrowing into a long leaf-stalk. The oval upper leaves have no stalks, their bases clasping the stem. The flowers are in open clusters of 7–15.

It lives on roadsides and grassy areas, and flowers from December to February.

The species name *coronaria* refers to the use of this plant for making garlands and crowns of flowers. In this and many other members of this family, the ovary ripens to form a hard-walled, upright capsule. When ripe this splits open at the top into five erect tooth-like parts. The seeds do not fall out of the open capsule unless the plant is disturbed in some way, for example, shaken by the wind or by a passing animal. Then the seeds are scattered from the capsule and, being very small and light, they are readily blown or carried some distance away from the parent plant.

*Malva sylvestris**
Large-flowered mallow

Malvaceae (Mallow Family)
25–40mm

A medium to tall, sparsely hairy perennial. The leaves are palmately lobed, cut less than two-thirds to the base, the lobes bluntly toothed. The flowers are in small clusters of two or more in the axils of the leaves. The petals are two to four times as long as the sepals.

Large-flowered mallow grows in waste places, roadsides, gardens and arable land. It is less common than other mallows but is more noticeable. It flowers from November to April.

Small-flowered mallow (*M. parviflora**) has petals 3–5mm long, only slightly longer than the sepals. Dwarf mallow (*M. neglecta**) is a prostrate annual with white to lilac flowers. Its petals are 8–15mm long, about twice as long as the sepals.

*Modiola caroliniana**
Creeping mallow

Malvaceae (Mallow Family)
10mm

A low, creeping annual with broad leaves deeply and palmately divided. In older plants, the leaf segments are often divided again pinnately into three to seven lobes. The orange to red flowers are conspicuous in spite of their relatively small size.

It grows in waste and coastal areas and flowers from October to May.

The Mallow Family is represented in this book by species of *Malva* (above) and *Modiola*. A distinctive feature of the flowers of this family is that there are many branched stamens. The filaments are fused together to form a tube which surrounds the style and is also fused to the petals. Cotton (*Gossypium*) is the most important plant of this family; the seeds of this genus have long hairs, from which cotton is spun. Another economically important plant is okra (ladies' fingers), a species of *Hibiscus* widely grown as a vegetable in the tropics and sub-tropics. Several other species of *Hibiscus* are cultivated in warmer regions as ornamental trees and shrubs. Other ornamental plants in this family include mallow, *Lavatera*, *Sidalcea*, and hollyhock.

63

The forget-me-nots

There are 40 species of forget-me-not in New Zealand, 34 of them native. All the native species are uncommon to rare, many being restricted to mountain areas or to one or two offshore islands. Most have white or yellow flowers. The two forget-me-nots described on this page are representative of the introduced species. One of the features of forget-me-nots, found also in several other members of the Borage family, is that the flowers are pink when they first open, turning blue after a day or two.

Myosotis scorpioides *
Water forget-me-not

Boraginaceae (Borage Family)
5–10mm

A short to medium perennial covered with short hairs pressed closely to the stem and sepals. The teeth of the calyx are one-third its length when the flower-bud opens. The ends of the petals are notched.

This species is common in wet places, flowering from November to May.

The name *scorpioides* refers to the way the inflorescence curls round like the tail of a scorpion. For this reason, the plant has also been called 'scorpion grass'. The other water forget-me-not, *M. laxa* *, is even more common, flowering from September. It has smaller flowers (2-5mm in diameter) and the teeth of the calyx are half its length when the buds open.

Myosotis sylvatica *
Garden forget-me-not

Boraginaceae (Borage Family)
6–10mm

A short to medium biennial or perennial covered with short, spreading hairs. The hairs on the sepals are hooked and the ends of the petals are rounded.

It is found as a garden escape, growing in waste places, roadsides and scrub, and as a garden weed. It flowers from November to March.

In the language of flowers, the forget-me-not means exactly what its name implies. It is said that, after the Battle of Waterloo in 1815, when the French army under Napoleon was defeated by Wellington, forget-me-nots grew up over the whole battlefield, in remembrance of the men who died there.

Navarretia squarrosa*
Californian stinkweed

Polemoniaceae (Phlox Family)
5–8mm

A hairy, sticky, unpleasant-smelling, stiff-stemmed annual of medium height. The stems branch near the base. The leaves are alternate and feathery. They soon fall from the plant, leaving the branches bare, with compact inflorescences at their tips. The flowers are in dense heads, with leafy bracts between them. The five sepals are fused into a tube, the short sepal tips ending in spines. There are four or five blue petals, fused to make a funnel-shaped tube only slightly longer than the calyx. The stamens are short, not projecting from the corolla tube.

Californian stinkweed is found on waste land, beside roads, and in other open habitats. It flowers from November to April.

This species is one of the less attractive members of its family. Some of the better known and more showy members of the family are garden plants such as *Phlox*, *Polemonium*, and *Cobaea*.

Neopaxia australasica
Neopaxia

Portulacaceae (Purslane Family)
20mm

A low, creeping and rooting, mat-forming, fleshy perennial, with flowering stalks up to 30mm long. The narrow leaves are fleshy and from 10 to 50mm long. The leaf-stalk is thin and wiry but is expanded into a papery sheath, which clasps the stem. The stems often have rounded corm-like swellings, and the roots may be swollen at intervals, looking like a string of beads. There are two free sepals and five white petals. The stamens are opposite the petals, as can be seen in the photograph. This feature helps to distinguish this species from similar white-flowered cushion-forming or mat-forming plants. Flowers are solitary or in a raceme of two or a few more.

It is a widespread plant, living beside streams and in other damp habitats, from the lowlands up to 2000m. It flowers from November to January.

This genus has also been known as *Claytonia* and as *Montia*.

Oenothera glazioviana*
Evening primrose

Onagraceae (Willowherb Family)
60–80mm

A tall, hairy biennial. Its stem is covered with dark red hairs with swollen bases. The flowers open in late afternoon or in the evening. The fruits are more or less cylindrical, but widening toward the base. Evening primrose is found in waste areas and on roadsides. It flowers from December to April.

The flowers of this plant are very short-lasting; perhaps it was this fact that led young Victorian men and women to send the evening primrose to lovers they suspected of being unfaithful. Sand primrose (*O. stricta**) has narrow leaves with finely and distantly toothed margins; the leaves are hairless except at the edges. The older petals become reddish orange. It is fragrant in the evenings. The fruits of *O. stricta* are more or less cylindrical, but narrow toward the base. The family includes several other plants with showy flowers, often grown in gardens: examples are fuchsia, *Clarkia*, and *Godetia*.

Ourisia macrocarpa
Ourisia

Scrophulariaceae (Foxglove Family)
20–30mm

A short, prostrate, almost hairless plant with rooting stems and erect inflorescence-stalks up to 700mm tall. The lower surfaces of the leaves, the leaf-stalks and the flowering stems are often dark purple. Flowers are in whorls; the photograph shows a whorl of eight open flowers and, above it on the stem, a whorl of seven unopened flower buds: above that is a third whorl of developing buds. The calyx lobes are broad and very bluntly tipped, sometimes slightly notched.

It grows in the South Island in damp habitats from 800m to 1300m. It flowers from October to May.

Unlike most genera of the Foxglove Family, the ourisias, hebes, and parahebes have almost regular flowers. The lower corolla lobe is only slightly larger than the others. There are 10 species of *Ourisia* native to New Zealand and all have similar flowers. A plant of similar appearance to *O. macrocarpa* is *O. macrophylla*, but this has narrow, tapering calyx lobes which are not notched, and has hairs on its leaf veins and elsewhere. It lacks the purple coloration.

66

Oxalis articulata*
Sourgrass

Oxalidaceae (Wood Sorrel Family)
20mm

A low to short, hairy perennial with leaves in basal rosettes. There are orange spots (calli) on the underside of the leaves and on the sepals. Leaflets are hairy above and below, unstalked, often unequal in size, divided into two rounded lobes. The flowers are in clusters of up to 35; flower stalks are curved back when the flowers are in bud, but become erect as the flowers open. Petals are rose, with darker veins, and pale pink on the outside.

This is a garden escape, established on roadsides and waste areas. It flowers from July to May.

Two similar plants with pink flowers are pink shamrock (*O. debilis**) and fishtail oxalis (*O. latifolia**). Both produce numerous small bulbs (bulbils) around a wide contractile root and are troublesome weeds. In pink shamrock, the leaflets are hairy below but not or scarcely hairy above; each leaflet has a hairy stalk about 1mm long. There are orange calli on the undersides of the leaves and on the sepals. In fishtail oxalis, the stalkless leaflets are divided into two tapering segments, giving a distinctive fishtail outline. The leaves have no hairs except for a few on the leaf-stalk and near the base of the leaf. There are no (or very small) calli on the leaves but there are two on each sepal.

Oxalis corniculata*
Horned oxalis

Oxalidaceae (Wood Sorrel Family)
4–7mm

A low to short perennial, with creeping, rooting stems. Leaves are alternate along the stem and without calli. The leaflets are very shortly stalked, equal in size, and usually, but not always, divided into two rounded lobes, 5–18mm long. Flowers are in clusters of one to five. The lower halves of the stalks of ripening fruits bend back, so there is a sharp angle about halfway along the stalks.

It lives on roadsides, waste and cultivated areas and flowers all the year round.

Another yellow-flowered oxalis is Bermuda buttercup (*O. pes-caprae**) with underground stems producing leaves and bulbils at its apex. Leaflets are unstalked, the terminal leaflet larger. The flowers are large (25–30mm).

Oxalis incarnata*   Oxalidaceae (Wood Sorrel Family)
Lilac oxalis   15–25mm

A low to short perennial, with a fleshy, contractile root and a bulb. The above-ground stem produces bulbils. Leaflets are more or less unstalked, divided by a broad cut into two rounded lobes, and have a row of orange calli beneath. The flowers are solitary, the sepals having two orange calli at their tips.

Lilac oxalis is found in gardens and waste areas, on banks, beneath hedges and in forest margins. It flowers all the year round.

Parahebe catarractae   Scrophulariaceae (Foxglove Family)
Parahebe   10mm

A short to medium sub-shrub with oval to lance-shaped, bluntly toothed leaves 10–40mm long. The inflorescences are long and many-flowered. The veining on the petals may be purple, as shown, or pink.

It lives in damp, rocky places, from sea level to 500m. It flowers from November to April.

The name *catarractae* comes from the Latin, meaning 'waterfall', referring to the fact that this species is commonly found near waterfalls. Usually the name of a species tells us something about what it looks like (for example: *erecta* = erect, p. 34); where it lives (*arvensis* = on cultivated land, p. 42), or where it comes from (*californica* = California, p. 54). Sometimes the species is named after a famous person, or the person who first collected it. *P. lyalli* is named after Dr. David Lyall who was a naturalist on several expeditions to New Zealand in the 1840s. Several other plants that he discovered are listed in this book. Several species (pp. 87, 90, 108) honour the Australian botanist Allan Cunningham, who visited New Zealand in the 1830s. Distinguished New Zealand botanists commemorated in this way include the Rev. William Colenso (pp. 23, 100), H. H. Allan (*Celmisia allanii*), author of Volume 1 of *Flora of New Zealand*, and T. F. Cheeseman who has a whole genus of alpine plants (*Cheesemania*) named after him.

Parahebe lyalli
Parahebe

Scrophulariaceae (Foxglove Family)
10mm

A low, creeping sub-shrub with oval to lance-shaped leaves, 5–10mm long, with two or three blunt teeth on each side. The leaves are fleshy and usually reddish. The inflorescences are long and many-flowered. Parahebe lives in damp, rocky places, from sea level to 1300m. It flowers from November to March. A similar plant, *P. decora*, has smaller leaves (1.5–4mm long), which are entire or have a single lobe near the base. The lower three flowers of the inflorescence are in a whorl, separate from the others.

Passiflora mollissima*
Banana passionfruit

Passifloraceae (Passion Flower Family)
✔ 40–50mm

A perennial climber, which reaches a height of several metres. Leaves are three-lobed, and the stipules are 5–10mm wide, wider than the stem (see photograph, top right). Showy, pink flowers hang downward. The style branches into three. Fruits are green at first, then ripen to dull yellow, looking like small, straight bananas.

It climbs on roadside shrubs, and flowers throughout the year.

The northern banana passionfruit (*P. mixta**) is common in north Auckland and a few other areas. It has larger flowers, and its stipules are only 2–4mm wide, about as wide as the stem. Black passionfruit (*P. edulis*) has tendrils to assist its climbing. Its leaves are dark green and shiny above. The fruit is purple when ripe. The fruits of all three species are edible. The sepals and petals are often similar, so that there appear to be 10 petals. The stamens are usually mounted on a central stalk arising from the base of the flower. Also on this stalk are numerous filaments, forming a radiating corona, and on the end of the stalk is the ovary. There is usually one style, which may be branched. Passionfruit are widely grown in tropical areas for the juicy fruit, which is also marketed as canned fruit juice and as a flavouring for ice cream.

Portulaca oleracea*
Purslane

Portulacaceae (Purslane Family)
✚ 6mm

A low to short, spreading annual, often with a pinkish tinge. The leaves are fleshy, oval and often tinged pink. The small, yellow flowers are in ones, twos or threes in the leaf axils, and are without stalks. As is typical in the Purslane Family, the flowers have two sepals, the lower one overlapping the upper one. The sepals are fleshy and hooded, and fall off at fruiting. The five yellow petals fall off soon after the flower opens. There are 6-15 stamens with yellow anthers. The style has three to six branches.

It grows on waste and cultivated land and flowers from November to March. The plant is rich in vitamin C and was at one time used to prevent scurvy.

Potentilla recta*
Tall cinquefoil

Rosaceae (Rose Family)
20–25 mm

A short to medium, shaggily hairy perennial with stiff, erect stems. The leaves are rounded and palmate; the lower leaves have five to seven deeply toothed leaflets. Epicalyx segments are narrowly lance-shaped, and the petals are longer than the sepals and deeply cut. The pale (sulphur) yellow of the petals distinguishes this from other cinquefoils. At first sight this might be taken to be a buttercup (see following pages), but the leaves of this plant have stipules, which are generally absent in the Buttercup Family.

It is found in the South Island, growing in dry locations in grassland, on roadsides and in waste areas. It flowers from December to May.

There are five other species of *Potentilla* in New Zealand, all with similar flowers, though with a richer yellow colour. Creeping cinquefoil (*P. anglica**) has smaller flowers with four or five petals, and has creeping, rooting stems. Hoary cinquefoil (*P. argentea**) has smaller flowers too, and the undersides of its leaves are silvery-white. Another creeping cinquefoil (*P. reptans**) has very long creeping stems. The native cinquefoil, *P. anserinoides*, is distinguished from the others by having pinnate leaves.

Phormium tenax
Harakeke, New Zealand flax

Phormiaceae (Harakeke Family)
✔ *m* 25-50mm long

Tall, perennial, tufted plants, with long (up to 3m) stiff, pointed leaves. The inflorescence is up to 5m or even 6m long, consisting of 50 or more dull red flowers; it produces dark, straight pods that are three-sided and erect when ripe.

This plant lives mainly in lowland swampy areas, and flowers in November and December.

Wharariki or mountain flax (*P. cookianum*) is similar but has yellow flowers. Its ripe pods are rounded in section, hang downward, and are spirally twisted. It lives in various places from coastal cliffs to high country. You may find it living beside *P. tenax*, and possibly forming hybrids.

Both species are visited by bellbirds, tuis and starlings, who feed on the nectar. The nectar was collected by the Maori for use as a drink and for sweetening. Fibres were extracted from the leaves and used for making textiles and cord. Sir Joseph Banks, on his visit to New Zealand in 1769 with Captain Cook, was impressed by the quality of the fibre. He wrote that it is 'of a strength superior to hemp . . . shining almost as silk'. The name *Phormium* comes from the Greek *phormion*, 'a mat', and refers to one of the practical uses of the leaf fibres.

Ranunculus bulbosus*
Bulbous buttercup

Ranunculaceae (Buttercup Family)
✗ 15–25mm

A short perennial growing from a swollen stem base, looking like a bulb. The stems are hairy, the hairs being pressed close to the stem. The leaves are divided into three deeply-toothed lobes, and the end lobe is stalked. The sepals are bent backward (see photograph) so that their tips are pressed closely to the flower-stalk.

It is found in damp areas, including pasture, waste ground and roadsides. It flowers from October to December.

Hairy buttercup (*R. sardous**) lacks the bulbous stem base, is more hairy than the bulbous buttercup, and the hairs spread out from the stem. Its flowers are pale yellow, and its fruits are flattened, with small, blunt swellings near the edges.

Ranunculus insignis
Korikori

Ranunculaceae (Buttercup Family)
20–30mm

A short, tufted perennial with entire, oval to circular leaves. The leaves are thick and hairy, usually on both surfaces. The margin has rounded teeth and is fringed with brown hairs. There are 2–10 flowers on a stem, and the flowers have five to seven petals.

Korikori grows in tussock grassland, scrub and rocky outcrops from 700m to 1800m. It flowers from November to February.

Ranunculus lyalli
Mount Cook lily, Great mountain buttercup

Ranunculaceae (Buttercup Family)
50–80mm

A short to tall, tufted perennial with circular, peltate leaves up to 400mm in diameter. The leaves are hairless on both surfaces and the margin has rounded teeth. There are 5–15 flowers on a stem, and they have 10–16 white petals.

This giant buttercup is found only in the South Island, growing beside streams and in other wet situations from 700m to 1500m. It flowers in December and January.

It is the largest-flowered buttercup in the world. The common name 'lily' is totally incorrect from the point of view of a botanist; the buttercup and lily families belong to two entirely distinctive plant groups.

The buttercups

Buttercups are all members of the genus *Ranunculus*, named from a Latin word meaning 'little frog': this refers to the fact that they tend to live in damp places. Some members of the genus (often called crowfoots) are fully aquatic, rooting in the beds of streams and having leaves specially adapted to being submerged in water.

The typical buttercup has five green sepals, five free yellow sepals, a large number of stamens, and a large number of carpels. There are exceptions; the number of petals varies and they may be white, as in two of the New Zealand species, *R. lyalli* (above) and *R. buchananii*. There is usually a small nectary scale inside each petal, at or near its base. Leaves are usually stalked and rounded in outline, though they are often deeply divided palmately into lobes or segments

*Ranunculus parviflorus**
Small-flowered buttercup

Ranunculaceae (Buttercup Family)
3–6mm

A short, hairy annual with rounded leaves partly cut into three to five deeply toothed lobes. The flower-stalk is grooved, with several flowers on each stalk. The sepals are bent backward, as in *R. bulbosus*, but the tips do not touch the flower-stalk. Petals and sepals are about the same length. Fruits are covered with hooked spines.

Small-flowered buttercup lives on waste ground, in tussock grassland and scrub, and also in gardens. It flowers from October to December.

*Ranunculus sceleratus**
Celery-leaved buttercup

Ranunculaceae (Buttercup Family)
5–15mm

This short to medium annual is hairless or sparsely covered with fine, closely-pressed hairs. Leaves are oval to kidney-shaped and look like celery leaves, being deeply cut into narrow lobes. There are up to 30 flowers on each stem. The boat-shaped sepals are turned slightly back. The fruiting head is cylindrical and bears several hundred fruits.

It grows in damp mud around ponds, on roadsides and on waste land. It flowers from October to February.

Spearwort (*R. flammula**) is a creeping perennial growing in wet situations. It has thick, fleshy stems, usually tinged with red. The leaves are simple; the lower leaves are oval or lance-shaped and the upper leaves are linear narrowly lance-shaped, with widely spaced shallow teeth on the margins. There are about 3–10 flowers, diameter 6–20mm, on a grooved flower-stalk. The name *flammula* means 'little flame', referring to the burning taste of its poisonous leaves.

Two common introduced buttercups

In great buttercup (*R. acris*) and creeping buttercup (*R. repens*) the sepals spread out beneath the petals. Great buttercup has rounded leaves, deeply three- to seven-lobed, the lobes being pinnately cut into narrow segments with pointed ends; the end lobe has no distinct stalk. The sepals have short, closely-pressed hairs. Creeping buttercup is identified by its stout, green runners which arch over close to the ground and take root at intervals. The lower leaves are divided into three stalked segments, each of which is divided again into three toothed lobes. These buttercups are poisonous to stock.

73

Rubus australis
Bush lawyer

Rosaceae (Rose Family)
8–15mm

A scrambling shrub with thorny stems. The leaves are palmate, usually with three or five leaflets, with small, reddish thorns. The terminal leaflet is oval to rounded, with the leaf-stalk longer than the leaflet, and with prickly teeth on each side. The flowers have either stamens or carpels, but not both. The photograph is of a male plant, which has only stamens in its flowers. Fruits are yellowish to orange.

It is found in lowland to montane forest and scrub, flowering from August to January.

Bush lawyers are well known to New Zealanders because of their painful thorns. Another bush lawyer is *R. cissoides,* in which the terminal leaflet is lance-shaped and the leaflet-stalk is usually much shorter than the leaflet. Fruits are orange to red.

Rubus fruticosus*
Blackberry, Bramble

Rosaceae (Rose Family)
✔ 20–30mm

A tall scrambling shrub with thorny stems and leaves. The tips of the stems arch over, rooting where they touch the soil. The leaves are usually trefoil, but some are pinnate, with five leaflets. Flowers are pink or white. Fruits, consisting of many fleshy, rounded segments, are red at first, ripening to black.

Blackberry can be found in a wide variety of habitats, from sea level to 1000m. It flowers from November to May.

Brought in by the early settlers as a fruit crop, the blackberry has escaped from cultivation and is so firmly established that in many places it ranks as a pest.

Edible fruits produced by the Rose Family include apple, pear, quince, medlar, cherry, plum, apricot, peach, nectarine, almond, raspberry, loganberry, boysenberry, strawberry and loquat. Hundreds of varieties of the genus *Rosa* have been bred with a diversity of form, colour and fragrance. Other popular flowering shrubs of this family include *Cotoneaster*, *Chaenomeles*, *Spiraea*, *Sorbus*, and *Pyracantha*.

74

Sagina procumbens*
Procumbent pearlwort

Caryophyllaceae (Pink Family)
4mm

A low, procumbent (lying on the ground), perennial plant. Its narrow leaves end in bristles. Petals are usually four in number, occasionally five (both forms can be seen in the photograph). They are much shorter than the sepals, and may be absent. The sepals spread out when the fruit ripens and, at the same time, the thin flower-stalks curl back on themselves.

This is widespread in a range of disturbed habitats, including lawns, from sea level to 1500m. It flowers from October to March.

Pearlwort (*S. apetala**) is a more upright plant, usually without petals. The sepals often have purplish margins. *S. subulata** usually has five petals and sepals, the petals and sepals being equal in length (about 2mm). A related plant is used as fodder for sheep, which is why this genus is named *Sagina*, the Latin for 'fodder'.

Scilla non-scripta*
Bluebell

Hyacinthaceae (Hyacinth Family)
15–20mm long

A short to medium perennial with long, narrow leaves growing from a bulb. The inflorescence is a short raceme of a few blue or white bell-shaped flowers. The tube of the flower is short and the ends of the six more-or-less identical tepals are curled back. The filaments of the six stamens, the stalks of the flowers, and the bracts at the base of the flower stalks are all the same colour as the flower.

The bluebell has become well established in grassy roadside areas. It flowers in September and October.

A related species, introduced into New Zealand from the Mediterranean region, is *S. peruviana**, which has inflorescences of smaller but more numerous flowers. *S. non-scripta* has both a bract and a bracteole (smaller) at the base of each flower stalk, as seen in the photograph, but *S. peruviana* has only a bract. The Elizabethans obtained starch from the bulbs and used it to stiffen the ruffs they wore around their necks. The sticky fluid from the stalks was used for gluing the pages of books and for fixing flight feathers to arrows.

Schizostylis coccinea*
Kaffir lily

Iridaceae (Iris Family)
50mm

A tall, evergreen perennial, with a tuft of leaves up to 300mm long, growing from a rhizome. The stems are stiff, up to 900mm long, bearing spikes of distinctive and brilliant red flowers. The lower parts of the tepals are fused into a narrow tube about 25mm long. The style is divided into three (sometimes four) fine, thread-like branches.

Cultivated in gardens because of its brilliant red flowers, it has escaped and is found in damp places beside roads, and in drains. It flowers from March to May.

Sedum acre*
Biting stonecrop, Wall pepper

Crassulaceae (Stonecrop family)
✗ 12mm

A low, creeping perennial. The leaves are thick, rounded in section, unstalked and not spreading. They have a burning taste (see below).

It grows on walls, banks, cliffs, sand, and shingle. It flowers from November to March.

This plant is poisonous, so do not swallow the leaf if you try tasting it. The name *Sedum* comes from the Latin for 'home': it was often grown on the roof of a house to protect it from lightning. White stonecrop (*S. album*) has smaller, white flowers. Its leaves are dark green, brownish green, or reddish green. They are thick, more or less rounded in section, but slightly flattened on the upper surface. They are not as close together as in biting stonecrop and they spread out widely from the stem. As their name suggests, stonecrops grow in dry, usually rocky places. Most members of the family have features associated with plants which live in such habitats: they have fleshy stems and leaves containing water-storage tissues. The stems are relatively short with the leaves clustered close together. The leaves usually have a waxy surface, to reduce evaporation of water. Several members of the family are cultivated as rock-garden plants or grown to cover stone or brick walls.

Sherardia arvensis*
Field madder

Rubiaceae (Bedstraw Family)
2–4.5mm

A low to short, spreading annual with square stems, its lower leaves elliptical and apparently in whorls of four. The upper leaves are lance-shaped, in whorls of five to six. The flowers are in few-flowered, rounded heads, surrounded by 8–10 leafy bracts.

Field madder lives in grassy places from sea level to 500m, and flowers all the year round.

The large leaf-like stipules of the members of the Bedstraw Family (see also *Galium*, p. 55) make it appear that the plant has whorls of leaves. Plants of economic importance in this family produce coffee, quinine (for the treatment of malaria) and ipecacuanha (an emetic). Among the ornamental garden plants are gardenia and coprosma. The trees and shrubs of the genus *Coprosma* are characteristic members of the New Zealand flora, there being about 45 species here, all except one of which are endemic.

Silene gallica*
Catchfly

Caryophyllaceae (Pink Family)
10–12mm

A short to medium annual, covered with long, sticky hairs. The flowers all point in the same direction, since the inflorescences are one-sided. Petals are notched at the tips, and are white or pink. The flowers have 10 stamens and three styles. The flower-stalks are 2–10mm long.

Catchfly is widespread on roadsides, cultivated land, waste land, coastal scrub and in gardens. It flowers from October to February.

A commonly found variety of catchfly (*S. gallica* var. *quinquevulnera**) has a dark red spot on each petal. Its variety name means 'five wounds', referring to the blood-like spots on the five petals. A species similar in appearance to *S. gallica**, found in the Wellington area, is *S. disticha**, which has the one-sided inflorescences arranged in pairs, with a single flower growing from the axil between them. Two common species of this genus have unisexual flowers, with either 10 stamens or five styles, but not both. These are red campion (*S. dioica**), which may also have pink flowers, and white campion (*S. latifolia**). Both have their flowers pointing in all directions.

Sisyrhinchium iridifolium *
Sisyrhinchium

Iridaceae (Iris Family)
20mm

A medium perennial with long leaves about 5mm wide. The six tepals are all alike, being creamy white and striped with purple. They have distinctively pointed tips. On the insides of the tepals the purple colouring forms a six-pointed 'star'. Outside, the tepals are veined in purple, and are hairy on the lower half.

Sisyrhinchium lives in grassy places and flowers in December.

There are two other distinct forms of this plant growing wild in New Zealand, which may be subspecies. One is described as *Sisyrhinchium* 'blue'*, and is a smaller plant with smaller (15mm diameter) blue flowers yellow-banded in the throat. The other is *Sisyrhinchium* 'yellow'*, with even smaller (6mm diameter) yellow flowers; it occurs only in the North Island.

Solanum laciniatum
Poroporo

Solanaceae (Nightshade Family)
✚ ✗ 40–50mm

A tall, hairless, soft-wooded shrub, the stems often with a purplish tinge. The leaves are entire or deeply and pinnately cut into one to four pairs of lobes. The tips of the corolla lobes are rounded, with a distinct notch.

Poroporo grows in and around forests, plantation and hedges. It flowers all the year round.

Another species, also known as poroporo, is *S. aviculare*. In this, the corolla lobes are broadly oval with pointed tips; they have no notch. Both species are now cultivated as sources of steroids. Although such substances are beneficial when administered in the correct, small dose, they are highly poisonous substances and plants containing them should always be treated with caution. Other members of this genus are important sources of food, especially the potato (*S. tuberosum*) and aubergine (egg-plant, *S. melongena*). Several other genera in the Nightshade Family are food sources, providing us with tomatoes, sweet peppers, tamarillos and Cape gooseberries. The family also includes a number of garden plants such as *Petunia*, *Nicotiana*, *Salpiglossis*, and *Schizanthus*. Many of these have escaped from cultivation and are now growing wild in New Zealand.

Solanum nigrum *
Black nightshade

Solanaceae (Nightshade Family)
✗ 10–13mm

A medium to tall annual or perennial of variable appearance. The stems are usually green, but they may be blackish. Leaves are broadly oval with a pointed tip, but the shape varies and they may be toothed or lobed and be slightly purplish in colour. The flowers are like those of the potato or tomato, with prominent, fused, yellow anthers. They are in loose clusters. The fruit of black nightshade is a rounded berry, green at first, usually turning black as it ripens.

Black nightshade grows in open areas, such as roadsides and waste ground. It flowers from October to May.

The plant may be poisonous, though probably only in its green parts, including the unripe fruits. Although the similarity in their common names is confusing, the highly poisonous plant *deadly* nightshade belongs to a different species and has a different appearance. Bittersweet (*S. dulcamara**) is a plant that may be confused with black nightshade, but it usually has bright purple petals (only occasionally white) and yellow anthers. Its berries are green at first, ripening to yellow, then to red. This species, too, is poisonous.

Spergula arvensis *
Spurrey

Caryophyllaceae (Pink Family)
4–8mm

A short to medium annual, covered with sticky hairs. The green to greyish green leaves are very narrow, with blunt tips, and apparently arranged in whorls of 10 or more. They are rounded in section with a narrow channel running along the underside. The sepals are oval, with glandular hairs and papery margins. The petals are almost equal in length to the sepals, possibly slightly longer, and are not notched at the tips. There are 5-10 stamens and five styles.

It lives mainly in dry places such as sand dunes, and on bare soil in gardens and by roadsides. It flowers from September to May.

*Stellaria graminea**
Stitchwort

Caryophyllaceae (Pink Family)
5–12mm

A short perennial with hairless, square stems. The opposite leaves have fused bases, surrounding the stem. The five petals are split to the base so that there appear to be 10 petals. They are equal to or rather longer than the sepals. The sepals have three distinct veins. There are up to 10 stamens and three styles.

It lives in damp places such as swamps, beside streams and in wet, grassy areas. It flowers from December to April.

Another square-stemmed stitchwort is bog stitchwort (*S. alsine**), with smaller flowers (4–6mm) and petals shorter than the sepals. Common chickweed (*S. media*) has round stems, with a distinct line of hairs running along them. The opposite leaves are not fused at the base. Petals are about equal in length to the sepals, which do not have distinct veins.

Symphytum x *uplandicum**
Russian comfrey

Boraginaceae (Borage Family)
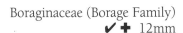 ✔ ✚ 12mm

A tall, roughly hairy, clump-forming perennial. The leaves are broadly spear-shaped, the blade of the leaf continuing into two narrow wings which run down the stem.

Found on roadsides and in waste places, it flowers from November to April.

Russian comfrey is a hybrid between common comfrey (*S. officinale**) and rough comfrey (*S. asperum**) both of which occur in New Zealand, but are uncommon. The species came from Uppland, in Sweden, which is presumably where the hybrid originated. In the Middle Ages, common comfrey was used as a remedy for broken bones; its name *Symphytum* comes from the Greek *symphysis* (growing together of bones) and *phyton* (a plant). Its species name *officinale* is one given to plants used in medicine — several other species in this book have been given this name. As well as being used as a curative, the leaves of common comfrey were eaten after being dipped in batter and fried.

Tetragonia trigyna
Beach spinach

Aizoaceae (Mesembryanthemum Family)
✔ 7mm

A short, spreading herb with fleshy leaves. The leaves are oval, rhomboid, or triangular in shape, and are alternate (unlike most members of this family). The flowers have no petals, the perianth consisting of four small, yellowish sepals. The flowers are usually solitary, but may occur in pairs.

It is found in coastal areas, on sand dunes and beaches, flowering from November to March.

The leaves of young plants are cooked and eaten. A related plant is kokihi, New Zealand spinach (*T. tetragonioides*).

Thelymitra venosa
Striped sun orchid

Orchidaceae (Orchid Family)
10–15mm long

A short to medium, hairless perennial, with a single narrow leaf, thickened at the edges and midrib. The blue flower, usually striped with a darker purplish blue, is not typical of orchids because its six tepals are very nearly identical in size, shape and colour. This is why the entry is in this section, but the other orchids are illustrated in the section dealing with irregular-shaped flowers. The tepals may occasionally be white.

It lives in wet, poorly drained areas and flowers from December to March.

The sun orchids are so named because their tepals open widely in bright sunshine. There are 12 species native to New Zealand, some with white, cream or pink flowers, and about half of them are endemic. The other blue-flowered sun orchids include: *T. formosa*, blue tepals without stripes or spots; *T. pulchella*, pinky-blue or white tepals with blue stripes (though it may also have plain pink tepals); *T. decora*, lavender-blue tepals with dark spots, mainly on the petals; and *T. ixioides*, blue tepals with darker blue spots. Probably the commonest wild orchid is *T. longifolia* (maikuku) in which the tepals are white, usually reddish green on the outside, and arranged in inflorescences of up to 10 blooms. The tubers of this orchid were eaten by the Maori, either raw or boiled.

Tradescantia fluminensis*
Wandering Jew

Commelinaceae (Spiderwort Family)
20mm

A medium, perennial herb, its trailing stems cover the ground in dense patches, taking root at intervals. The leaves are broad and oval, as can be seen in the photograph; this is unusual for leaves with parallel veins. The bases of the leaves curl round to form sheaths surrounding the stem.

Wandering Jew is found in damp, shady places, often overgrowing the local vegetation. In many places it is regarded as a noxious plant. It flowers in December and January.

The name 'wandering Jew', descriptive of the ease with which this plant spreads, is also applied to some other members of this family. The popular house plant, *Zebrina pendula*, with purple flowers and leaves often striped white, green and purple, is another wandering Jew. The hairs on the stamens make an interesting subject for a low-power microscope: if mounted in water, the hairs can be seen to consist of exceptionally large cells. It is usually possible to see the living material inside the cells (nucleus and cytoplasm) slowly and continuously circulating.

Verbascum thapsus*
Woolly mullein, Aaron's rod

Scrophulariaceae (Foxglove Family)
15–25mm

A tall, sturdy, annual or biennial plant, covered with dense, woolly felt and with an erect, unbranched stem growing from a basal rosette. It can grow up to 3m tall. Stem leaves are broadly oval and bluntly toothed, their bases running down to form wings on the stem. There are five stamens, three with a tuft of white hairs and two without hairs.

It lives in dry locations, beside roads, on riverbeds, on poor pastures and on dry, loose soils. It flowers from July to April.

The name 'Aaron's rod' refers to the rod of the biblical Aaron, 'which was budded and brought forth buds and bloomed blossoms'. In early times the plant was dipped in tallow and used as a torch plant. Its large felty leaves were used to line shoes.

Verbascum virgatum *
Moth mullein

Scrophulariaceae (Foxglove Family)
25–40mm

A tall, sturdy, biennial plant, moderately hairy, with an erect, unbranched stem growing from a basal rosette. It can grow up to 2m tall. Stem leaves are oval, toothed and more or less hairless. The upper stem leaves are narrower, but with lobes near the base, clasping the stem. There are five stamens, with purple or violet hairs, the two upper stamens sometimes with white hairs.

It lives in open, disturbed areas and flowers from November to May.

The same species may be given quite different common names in different parts of the world. The verbascums are an example of this. *V. virgatum* is called moth mullein in New Zealand, but in Europe the same name is given to another species, *V. blattaria*. There, *V. virgatum* is called twiggy mullein. *V. blattaria* grows in New Zealand too, but here its common name is white mullein. This is all very perplexing and is the reason why we have always identified species by their scientific names in this book.

Vinca major *
Greater periwinkle

Apocynaceae (Periwinkle Family)
35–40mm

A short, creeping perennial with shallow rhizomes and green stems up to 2m long, woody at the base, rooting at the tip, and then turning up. The leaves are opposite and evergreen, usually dark green but variegated forms are sometimes found. It forms a mat covering large areas. The flowers are solitary, with distinctive, square-cut petals, their limbs spreading out in a saucer-shaped disc. The sepals are more than 7mm long, distinguishing this species from the lesser periwinkle, *V. minor*, in which the sepals are less than 5mm long.

Greater periwinkle grows on waste land and by roadsides, often escaping from gardens where it is grown as a ground cover. It grows well under trees and shrubs, and may become a troublesome weed in reserves. It flowers all the year round.

Wahlenbergia gracilis
Rimu-roa

Campanulaceae (Bellflower Family)
15–20mm

A short or medium, annual to perennial herb with a tap root, giving rise to slender, much-branched stems. Basal leaves are usually in a rosette, spoon-shaped to narrowly oval. The upper leaves are narrower and may be opposite. The upper stem and calyx are hairless. The flower-stalk is long, unbranched or slightly branched. The flowers have a short tube; the petals are sometimes dark blue, as shown in the photograph, but they may be paler, or white.

Rimu-roa lives in lowland and sub-alpine grassland and flowers from September to April.

Harebell (*W. albomarginata*) has a branching rhizome, each branch ending in a rosette of spoon-shaped or spear-shaped leaves. The leaves are up to 20mm long, often purplish, and have thickened, white margins. A thin flower-stalk up to 250mm long grows from each rosette, ending in a solitary flower. The calyx lobes are much shorter than the corolla tube. Flowers are white or bluish white, often with veins of darker blue. The size of the leaves and length of the flower-stalk are very much reduced in dry habitats.

Watsonia ardernei*
Watsonia

Iridaceae (Iris Family)
35–45mm

A tall, robust perennial growing in clumps from corms about 40mm in diameter. The leaves are broad and sword-shaped, with yellowish margins. Its inflorescence of white flowers branches freely. The tube of the flower is a broad funnel. The style branches into three and each branch is shortly branched again into two.

It is a garden escape, living in grassy places. It flowers in October and November.

Another very common garden escape is *W. bulbillifera** with salmon-pink or brick-red flowers. Its corm is 70mm in diameter. The inflorescence is less branched than in *W. ardernei* and often not branched at all. It is distinguished from the other watsonias by the numerous, small, reddish-brown shining corms (bulbils) produced instead of flowers.

Irregular-shaped flowers

Adenochilus gracilis
Adenochilus orchid

Orchidaceae (Orchid Family)
10–15mm

A low to short perennial with a single, oval green leaf, about 10–30mm long, usually about half-way up the stem. There are also two to three short, narrow bracts. The lateral tepals are alike in shape and greenish white. The central sepal is deeply hooded, covering the column and tongue, which is short and broad, spotted or striped with red, and with a distinctively sharp-pointed, curved tip. The tongue also bears a row of yellowish calli (small swellings) which extends on to the tip.

It is common in light shade and flowers from May to September.

As in almost all orchid flowers, the pollen is produced in waxy masses, called *pollinia*. When a pollinating insect visits a flower, a whole pollinium is transferred to its body. The insect then visits another flower, where the pollinium is transferred to the stigma.

Aporostylis bifolia
Odd-leaved orchid

Orchidaceae (Orchid Family)
15–25mm

A short, hairy perennial, reproducing by tubers. At the bottom of the stem are two soft hairy leaves; the lower leaf is longer and broader than the upper one, and both are blotched with brown. At the top of the single stem is a white, sometimes pink, flower. The petals have a pink stripe down the middle. The middle petal is wider than the others, arched over to form a shallow hood. The tongue is broad and oval, with two rows of yellow calli (see above) near the base. The tongue has fallen from the flower in the left of the photograph, revealing the column which has two narrow wings running up either side of it, becoming broader and forming two lobes, one on each side of the anther.

It lives in wet areas, such as bogs and hollows in grassland and scrub, flowering in December and January.

Caladenia lyalli
White fingers

Orchidaceae (Orchid Family)
15–25mm

A short, slightly hairy perennial, with a single, slightly hairy leaf up to 8mm wide. Flowers are white or pink. The tongue has three lobes: the middle lobe is triangular, its tip curled tightly back; the two broad side lobes are turned upward, with reddish stripes. There are four rows of yellow calli (p. 85) on the central area of the tongue.

Found in beech forest, scrub and grassland, flowering from November to February.

C. carnea has a single leaf (up to 4mm wide) with both short, glandular hairs and long, non-glandular hairs. It has yellowish calli on the edges of the tip of the tongue, and two rows of red, yellow-tipped calli on the centre of the tongue. It flowers in September and October.

Centranthus ruber *
Spur valerian

Valerianaceae (Valerian Family)
✔ 4–8mm

A medium to tall, greyish green perennial, the stems branching from the base of the plant. The leaves are opposite. They are simple, oval in shape with pointed tips. The upper leaves may be toothed near the base; they are stalkless and they clasp the stem. The lower leaves are untoothed and have stalks. The flowers are fragrant, coloured red, pink or white, and massed in showy branched clusters. The corolla is of five joined petals, their tips spreading out, with the two lower ones smaller than the others. The petals tube is spurred at the base. There is only one stamen.

It lives on banks, cliffs, retaining walls, roadsides and waste areas. It flowers from November to June.

The leaves have a bitter taste but, if cut young, they can be eaten as salad. The family includes cornsalad (*Valerianella carinata*) which is cultivated for its leaves. This has escaped from cultivation; it has very small, unspurred, pale blue flowers, with three stamens.

Corybas rivularis
Spider orchid

Orchidaceae (Orchid Family)
10mm

A low-growing perennial with a single, broad, flat green leaf. The single, short-stalked flower is below the leaf. The lateral tepals are narrow and elongated, hence the name 'spider orchid'. The stalkless leaf is longer than broad, with wavy edges. It is heart-shaped at the base and tapers gradually to a sharply angled apex. The central sepal of *C. rivularis* is much longer than in the two other species described here, tapering to a long, narrow point.

It lives on the forest floor, flowering from September to November.

C. macranthus has an oval fleshy leaf, silvery below, about 35mm long on a relatively long stalk. The apex of the leaf is rounded, but has a minute, pointed tip. The flower is dark red and white with prominent 'spider's legs'. The tongue is longer than the central sepal, broad and curved back, edged with small teeth. *C. trilobus* has a rounded leaf, about 20mm in diameter on a relatively long stalk. The tip is sharply pointed with rounded lobes on either side. The flower is red and green with prominent white 'spider's legs'. The tongue is curved back, hidden in the hood, and its edge has many small teeth.

Dendrobium cunninghamii
Lady's slipper orchid

Orchidaceae (Orchid Family)
20–25mm

A short perennial with yellow cane-like stems up to 1.5m long, with many drooping branches. The leaves are well spaced out along the stem and are narrow (30–50mm long, 3mm wide). The flowers are larger than those of most orchids, and occur in clusters of up to six. The tongue has three lobes: the central lobe is broad and white; the two side lobes are red, and stand up. The base of the tongue has four to five yellowish ridges on it.

Lady's slipper grows as an epiphyte on trees in well lit areas of forest, also on fallen logs and on rocks. It flowers from December to February.

This is the southernmost member of the large and showy *Dendrobium* genus. The name *Dendrobium* comes from the Greek *dendron* (a tree) and *bios* (life), referring to its habit of living on trees.

Digitalis purpurea *
Foxglove

Scrophulariaceae (Foxglove Family)
✚ ✗ 35–50mm long

A tall biennial or perennial with a single, erect stem topped with a conspicuous raceme of flowers, the flowers being to one side of the stalk. The leaves are broadly lance-shaped, wrinkled and soft to the touch, with a felted under-surface. The five-lobed calyx is about as long as the two-lipped corolla tube, which is pinkish purple; it has white spots ringed with darker purple at its lower end. Flowers may also be white.

Foxglove lives in open, disturbed areas, and may often be seen flourishing on hillsides. It flowers from October to January.

This is the only member of this large family which is of economic importance. *Digitalis* is the source of the alkaloid digitalin, a highly poisonous substance used in very small doses to treat heart disease. The foxglove is also grown as an ornamental plant.

Earina autumnalis
Raupeka, Easter orchid

Orchidaceae (Orchid Family)
13mm

A medium perennial with short, erect stems, drooping if the plant grows longer (up to 1m), but usually unbranched. The leaves are 40–120mm long, 5–8mm wide, densely covering the stems. The showy inflorescence of up to 40 waxy, white, fragrant flowers distinguishes this species from *E. mucronata* which has a drooping spray of up to 10 greenish cream flowers. The sepals are alike in being triangular in shape, and about the same length as the more rounded lateral petals. The base of the tongue is yellow, and its sides curve up to partly enclose the column.

The plant is epiphytic on trees, but also grows on rocks and banks. It flowers from February to April, so is often in bloom at Easter. The leaves of *E. mucronata* are longer (60–150mm) and narrower (4–6mm) and the leaf sheaths have small, dark spots. The tongue is broader and longer than that of *E. autumnalis* and is yellowish, its tip being expanded into a broad lobe that projects from the flower.

Euphrasia cuneata
Tutumako

Scrophulariaceae (Foxglove Family)
15–20mm long

A medium, perennial plant. The lower parts of the stems are woody. It has oval to broadly oval, hairless, short-stalked leaves; these have one to three blunt teeth on each margin. The lower lip of the corolla is much larger than the upper lip. There are four stamens (one pair with longer filaments than the other pair) and the anthers are reddish brown.

It lives in open rocky locations and in scrub from sea level to 1500m, flowering from January to April.

Eyebright, *E. zelandica,* is a low, fleshy, annual plant with stalkless leaves, two to five narrow, pointed teeth on each margin. The leaves are clustered in rosettes at the ends of the stems, surrounding the short-stalked or stalkless flowers. The flowers are smaller (6–10mm long), white, with yellow in the throat. Anthers are yellow to golden brown.

Fumaria muralis*
Scrambling fumitory, Wall fumitory

Fumariaceae (Fumitory Family)
8–10mm long

A short, annual plant with a weak stem. The leaves are alternate, light bluish green in colour, and deeply cut into many wedge-shaped or lance-shaped segments. The racemes have up to 15 flowers, the stalk of the raceme being longer than the raceme itself. There are two sepals, which fall off soon after the flower opens. The flowers are two-lipped, with spurs at the bases of the petals. The lower petal is spoon-shaped and its edges are turned up. The tips of the petals are dark purple. The fruits are slightly longer than broad, smooth when dry.

It is a common plant in cultivated and waste areas where it flowers from September to March.

The raceme stalk of fumitory (*F. officinalis**) is shorter than the raceme. The plant has smaller flowers, the lower petal being spoon-shaped, with a wide-spreading margin at its tip. The tips of the petals are purple and dark green. The fruits are slightly broader than long, rough when dry.

Gastrodia cunninghamii
Huperei, Perei, Maukuuku, Black orchid   ✔ *m* 14mm long

Orchidaceae (Orchid Family)

A tall leafless plant with brown stems, bearing a spike of purplish brown flowers. The flowers are tubular with five lobes. The tongue is enclosed in the tube and has wavy edges. The flowers are mottled with lighter swollen spots, a feature that distinguishes this from other species of *Gastrodia*. The inside of the flowers is creamy white.

It is found in lowland forests and flowers from November to February.

The roots were used by the Maori as winter food (perei). *G. sesamoides* lives in open forest and scrub, north of latitude 42° S. Both species obtain nourishment from soil fungi that live as parasites on the roots of forest trees. The other orchids, too, associate with fungi, but not with parasites. They have a sheath of fungus threads covering their roots. The fungus grows out into the soil, absorbing mineral nutrients, some of which it passes on to the orchid. In return, the fungus receives photosynthesised materials from the orchid.

Lamium purpureum *
Red dead-nettle

Lamiaceae (Mint Family)
10–14mm long

A low to medium, downy annual, with broad, heart-shaped, bluntly toothed, stalked leaves. There is a ring of hairs inside the corolla tube, near the base.

It grows on waste and cultivated land and flowers from September to November.

Cut-leaved dead-nettle (*L. hybridum**) is similar to red dead nettle but its leaves are irregularly and more deeply toothed, and it lacks the ring of hairs in the corolla tube. Its leaves are broad and rounded, often almost kidney-shaped. The lower lip of the corolla has a large middle lobe, divided into two, and two small side lobes. It flowers from June to December.

Henbit (*L. amplexicaule**), a closely related plant, is so called because the coarsely rounded teeth make the stalked leaves look as if they have been bitten by hens. Its distinctive feature is that leaf-like bracts in the inflorescence are unstalked and the bases of opposite bracts are fused together, completely surrounding the inflorescence stalk.

90

*Lathyrus latifolius** *
Everlasting pea

Fabaceae (Pea Family)
20–30mm long

A climbing, hairless perennial with winged stems. The stipules are lance-shaped, pointed at either end, usually as wide as or wider than the stem. The leaves are parallel-veined, with one pair of leaflets, the remaining leaflets being modified into tendrils. The inflorescence consists of 5–15 flowers, with typical pea-flower structure. The seeds have a wrinkled surface.

Everlasting pea is common in waste places, where it flowers from September to May.

This is a relative of the sweet pea, *L. odoratus*, often grown in gardens for its showy flowers and pleasant scent.

*Lathyrus tingitanus** *
Tangier pea

Fabaceae (Pea Family)
20–35mm long

A climbing, hairless annual with winged stems. The stipules are lance-shaped and pointed at each end. The leaves are parallel-veined, with one pair of leaflets, the remaining leaflets being modified into tendrils. The inflorescence consists of one to three flowers, with typical pea-flower structure. The seeds have a smooth surface.

It is common in waste places and flowers from August to May.

The pea family

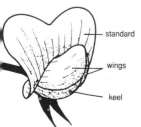

standard

wings

keel

This family is also known as the Leguminosae, after the typical 'pea-pod' fruit, the legume, or as the Papilionaceae, after the butterfly-like appearance of the flowers of many genera. The petals comprise a (usually) large standard petal, two wing petals and two keel petals. The keel petals are usually fused along their adjacent edges and enclose the 10 stamens. The filaments of the stamens may be free, or nine of them may be fused to form a tube around the single superior ovary. One stamen remains free so that the tube is not complete.

Lobelia anceps
Lobelia

Lobeliaceae (Lobelia Family)
6–10mm long

A low, spreading, hairless herb with narrowly winged stems. The leaves vary in shape and thickness and may be quite fleshy, like those in the photograph, or thin like a more typical leaf. The lower leaves are broader and more rounded than the upper leaves, which are narrow and strap-shaped. The lower leaves have flat leaf-stalks, while the upper leaves are stalkless. The margins of the leaves are entire or have shallow, widely-spaced teeth.The margins run down into the wings on the stems. In some plants all leaves are alike. The flowers are on short stalks in the axils of the upper, narrow leaves, and may be white, pale blue or pale pink. The corolla tube is split to the base along one side.

It lives mainly in coastal areas, on sand and rocks, and flowers from September to May.

Bedding lobelia (*L. erinus**) is a garden escape with trailing stems and variable leaves. Sometimes they are broader than those shown in the photograph, and occasionally spoon-shaped. Their margins may be toothed or entire. The corolla tube is split to the base on the upper side. Bedding lobelia was the subject of experiments by Charles Darwin. He found that bees did not visit flowers if the blue petals were cut off, showing that bees locate flowers by sight, not by smell.

It is common in waste places; flowers from August to May.

*Lonicera japonica**
Japanese honeysuckle

Caprifoliaceae (Honeysuckle Family)
20–45mm long

An evergreen or semi-evergreen climber with purplish stems; the leaves produced in spring are more deeply lobed than those shown in the photograph. The calyx consists of five small, equal sepals, joined together. The corolla is two-lipped, the upper lip being four-toothed and the lower lip entire. The lower lip curls strongly backward. The flowers are white when they open, but later become yellow.

Honeysuckle escapes on to roadsides near habitation, and flowers from September to May.

Lotus pedunculatus*
Lotus

Fabaceae (Pea Family)
10–13mm long

A low to medium perennial with hollow stems and pinnate leaves. There are two pairs of oval leaflets, with distinct side veins. Leaves are unstalked, with no stipules, so that the lower pair of leaflets can be mistaken for large stipules. The inflorescence of 5–12 flowers is on a stalk much longer than the leaves; the flowers are short-stalked, in an umbel-like head. The teeth of the calyx are equal to or less than the length of the calyx tube.

It is found in waste areas and pastures, and in damp habitats: flowers from November to January.

L. tenuis* has rather narrower leaflets with only the main vein clearly visible, more or less solid stems and two to four flowers in the inflorescence. Hairy birdsfoot trefoil (*L. suaveolens*) is a shaggily hairy, lotus-like perennial. The teeth of the calyx are longer than the calyx tube. Lotus is used as a pasture plant, and to stabilise the edges of newly made roads.

Lupinus arboreus*
Tree lupin

Fabaceae (Pea Family)
15–18mm long

A tall, hairy shrub with palmate leaves, of 5–11 leaflets, 3–10mm wide. The inflorescence is a raceme of yellow, white or blue-tinged, sweetly scented flowers.

Tree lupin is common in sandy areas, particularly near or on the coasts where it flowers from October to May.

The Russell lupin (*L. polyphyllus*) has larger leaves of 8–15 leaflets, 10-30mm wide. These plants are garden escapes and have a variety of colours, including many which are bi-coloured. This species is commoner in the South Island, being found only in the Wellington area in the North Island. Lupins are pollinated by the larger (and heavier) bees. The sticky pollen is retained inside the tube formed by the fused filaments (p. 91). When a bee lands on the keel, its weight forces the keel down, exposing the end of the stamen tube. A quantity of pollen is extruded on to the underside of the bee's abdomen. When the bee visits another, more mature, lupin flower, the stigma picks up pollen from the same area of the abdomen.

Mazus radicans
Mazus

Scrophulariaceae (Foxglove Family)
12–20mm long

A low, creeping perennial. Its rhizome produces short, upright branches, with usually hairy but sometimes hairless, oval, entire leaves. The dark markings on the edges of the leaves are a distinctive feature of this plant. The two-lipped flowers are typical of the foxglove family with their fused petals. The four stamens grow from the inside of the corolla tube, two on shorter filaments than the others; this too is a feature of most members of this family. There are up to three flowers on each flower stalk.

Mazus grows in swamps, bogs and damp, grassy areas, from sea level to 1200m. It flowers from November to March.

The other New Zealand native species is *M. pumilio*. It has smaller flowers (6–12mm long), which may occasionally be blue, and occur in clusters of up to six. The name *Mazus* comes from the Greek *mazos* (teat), referring to the prominent swellings at the base of the petals.

Medicago arabica*
Spotted bur medick

Fabaceae (Pea Family)
4–6mm long

A low, prostrate, almost hairless annual, with trefoil leaves, each leaflet having a dark spot at its centre. The inflorescence has one to four flowers. The pod is coiled into a spiral of three to seven turns, has a double row of spines, and faint net-veining.

It grows in waste places, pastures and lawns, and flowers from September to April.

A similar species is bur medick (*M. nigra**), with unspotted leaflets, and distinctly net-veined pods. The trefoil leaf is a distinctive feature of medicagos, clovers and melilots (sweet clovers) as well as some other members of this family. It may be thought of as a pinnate leaf which has only the terminal leaflet and one pair of lateral leaflets. A distinguishing feature of the medicks is the pod which, when mature, is tightly coiled into a spiral, usually of several turns. In some species it bears large, many-branched spines, often with hooked tips, as an aid to dispersal of the fruits, tangled in the coats of animals.

*Medicago lupulina**
Black medick

Fabaceae (Pea Family)
2–3mm long

A low, prostrate, hairy annual, with trefoil leaves, each leaflet ending in a tiny point. It has an inflorescence of 10–15 flowers in a rounded head. The petals fall off immediately after flowering. The pod is coiled in about one turn, and is hairy, but has no spines.

It grows in waste places, in pastures and on coastal sites, flowering from November to May.

*Medicago sativa**
Lucerne

Fabaceae (Pea Family)
7–12mm long

A medium, slightly hairy perennial with trefoil leaves. The inflorescence is a short raceme of violet, blue, or sometimes white flowers. The pods are coiled in a tight spiral of up to three turns.

It grows on waste and cultivated areas, and flowers from November to May.

Lucerne has been grown as a fodder crop since early in the history of agriculture. It is now grown widely in all temperate parts of the world. Clover and sainfoin are two other members of this family grown as forage. The Fabaceae provide food for humans too, and are second only to the Grass Family in this respect. Examples are: peas, beans (many kinds), lentils, groundnuts (peanuts), Moreton Bay chestnuts (dried, roasted and eaten by Australian aborigines). All these have high protein content. The groundnut is also a source of oil. Other economically important members of this family include the indigo plant, liquorice and timbers such as wattle, rose-wood, and Brazil-wood (used for making violin bows). Probably the most important plant in the family is the soya bean (*Glycine max*). It is a source of oil for cooking, and for making margarine, as well as soap making, paint and plastics. Soya bean sprouts are a major feature of Chinese cuisine. Soya flour has a high protein content and is used in the manufacture of ice cream, milk substitutes and soy sauce.

Mentha x *piperita* var. *citrata* *
Lemon mint, Bergamot mint

Lamiaceae (Mint Family)
♥ 5–6mm long

A short to medium, hairy perennial with a pleasant, lemony smell. The leaves have distinct stalks and sharply pointed teeth. The inflorescence is dense and elongated, with a rounded head of flowers and a few rounded clusters of flowers below.

Lemon mint lives in and around streams, rivers and lakes. It flowers from January to May.

This is a hybrid of water mint, *M. aquatica*, and spearmint, *M. spicata* (see below). The ancient Greeks used it for making perfumes. They dried and powdered the plants, sprinkling the powder on their beds. The other variety is *piperita* *, or peppermint. It has narrower leaves and a long tapering inflorescence. The Romans used to flavour their wine with this mint. In those days, wine was only for gods and men, and women were liable to the death penalty if caught drinking it. Many women made a paste of mint and honey, which they chewed to mask the smell of wine that they had drunk in secret.

Mentha pulegium *
Pennyroyal

Lamiaceae (Mint Family)
✔ ♥ 4–6mm long

A short perennial with a strong smell. The leaves are oval with entire or slightly toothed margins. The inflorescence has no terminal head, but consists of several, separated, dense whorls of flowers.

It lives in pastures and beside rivers and lakes. It flowers from November to May.

In ancient times the plants were spread on the floor to keep away mice and fleas (Latin *pulices*). It was also used as a stuffing for black pudding in the north of England, where it was known as 'pudding grass'.

The inflorescences of spearmint, *M. spicata*, are narrow and tapering, like spires. This is what gave it its original name of 'spire mint'. Spearmint has a distinctive 'mint sauce' smell. There are two subspecies. Subspecies *spicata* * is more or less hairless. Subspecies *tomentosa* * has long, soft grey hairs on the stem and leaves.

Microtis unifolia
Onion orchid

Orchidaceae (Orchid Family)
3mm long

A tall, hairless perennial, with a single rolled leaf, often reaching higher than the top of the inflorescence, which is a raceme up to 30cm long, though usually shorter. The raceme consists of many small, densely packed flowers with green tepals. The uppermost sepal (the dorsal sepal) is formed into a hood (compare with *Prasophyllum*). The tongue is broad, roughly rectangular, with an irregular outline and a notch at its tip.

Widespread in open places, it flowers from October to February.

Mimulus guttatus*
Monkey musk

Scrophulariaceae (Foxglove Family)
30–45mm long

A short, mainly hairless perennial with broad, opposite, roundly toothed leaves. The bases of the upper pairs of leaves are fused, clasping the stem. The flower is distinguished by the small, bright red spots at its mouth, though these are sometimes absent. The throat of the flower is more or less closed by a pouch formed from the upper lip of the corolla.

Monkey musk is common in wet places such as swamps, stream banks and ditches. It flowers from November to March.

The flower is said to resemble a monkey's face, which gives it its common name, monkey musk. Because it *mimics* a monkey it is given its genus name, *Mimulus*. A related plant, musk (*M. moschatus*) is a short, stickily hairy perennial with broad, opposite, distantly toothed or entire leaves. The upper leaves clasp the stem. The flowers are bright yellow and the tube is marked with thin, dark veins but there are no spots. They are smaller than those of *M. guttatus*. The pouch is absent so the throat of the flower is open. At one time, musk was cultivated for its scent. In the early 20th century, unscented plants began to appear and today no scented plants are known.

Orobanche minor*
Broomrape

Orobanchaceae (Broomrape Family)
10–18mm long

A short to medium annual, with a straight, un-branched stem bearing yellowish scale-leaves and a spike of pale yellowish flowers. The plants may also be purplish.

It is found as a parasite on plants of pastures and crops, on roadsides and in waste areas. It flowers from August to January.

All members of this family are parasitic on the roots of other plants. They lack the green pigment chlorophyll, so they may be whitish or variously coloured in light brown or purple. Since they are parasitic, they have no need to produce food materials by photosynthesis. This means that they do not need chlorophyll, and their leaves are reduced to scales. Broomrape produces large quantities of dust-like seeds, which accounts for its success as a weed. The smallness of the seeds may be related to the fact that, during the early stages of its development, the broomrape plant can absorb food materials from the plant on which it is a parasite. Unlike the seedlings of normal plants, the broomrape seedlings do not rely on having a massive store of food in the seed, produced by their parents. *O. minor* is parasitic on clovers, but is also found on other plants. Many other species of *Orobanche* parasitise only one host species.

Parentucellia viscosa*
Tarweed

Scrophulariaceae (Foxglove Family)
8–12mm

A medium annual, with an erect, unbranched stem and lance-shaped, opposite, toothed leaves, 12–45mm long. The leaves and stems are covered with sticky hairs. The calyx is 10–15mm long, with five teeth. The corolla is two-lipped, the upper lip hooded, the lower lip longer and spreading, with three lobes.

Tarweed is common in damp pastures, on roadsides and in waste areas. It flowers from November to May.

This plant is semiparasitic on the roots of other plants, but it has leaves with chlorophyll, so is able to photosynthesise at least part of its requirements itself.

*Parochetus communis**
Shamrock pea

Fabaceae (Pea Family)
18–22mm long

A prostrate perennial with trefoil leaves and pea-like flowers (see p. 91) of a distinctive blue colour.

It grows in waste places, especially where is it damp and shady. Flowers from December to September.

The trefoil leaves of this plant differ from those of the clovers and medicks (p. 94), which are *pinnate* leaves with the lateral leaflets reduced to one pair. Although the trefoil leaves of *Parochetus* have almost the same appearance, they are considered to be *palmate* leaves (as in lupin), but with only three segments.

Pelargonium x *asperum**
Geranium

Geraniaceae (Geranium Family)
15–20mm

A medium to tall, hairy, strongly aromatic sub-shrub. The leaves are triangular, deeply cut into three lobes with toothed, wavy margins. The side lobes each have a sub-lobe, while the terminal lobe has two sub-lobes. The inflorescence is an umbel of about 10 flowers on a relatively long stalk. The upper sepal has a spur, joined to the flower-stalk. The two upper petals are larger than the three lower petals and have distinctive markings. The style and stigmas are rose-coloured.

This is a common garden escape and is most often found in coastal areas. It flowers throughout the year.

Several other hybrids are widely cultivated in gardens and have escaped. Nutmeg geranium (*P. 'fragrans**) is a bushy plant smelling of nutmeg; its upper two petals have crimson markings. Regal pelargonium (*P.* x *domesticum**) has triangular to broadly oval leaves, and purplish or dark crimson markings on the upper petals, including a central patch. Zonal pelargonium (*P.* x *hortatum**) is recognised by the dark ring on its leaves. The native pelargonium *P. inodorum* is a non-aromatic, scrambling, hairy plant with rounded, usually unlobed leaves and smaller, pink or rose flowers. It has purple streaks on the upper two petals.

Prasophyllum colensoi
Leek orchid

Orchidaceae (Orchid Family)
7mm long

A short, hairless perennial with a single, long, rolled leaf, often reaching higher than the raceme of flowers. The raceme consists of many small, fleshy, reddish green or yellowish green flowers. The flower is 'upside down' when compared with most other orchid flowers, so there are *two* partly fused lateral sepals *above* the flower. The central sepal is *below* the flower and is slightly curved, but not hooded. The tongue tapers to a narrow tip, with a single callus (p. 85) extending almost as far as the tip.

Widespread in grassland, especially where it is damp or boggy. It flowers from November to February.

There are three other species of *Prasophyllum* that are reasonably common in New Zealand. *P. patens*, found only in the North Island, has the long, rolled leaf of *P. colensoi*, but the tongue is wider, with a wavy tip, and has no callus at the tip. The other two species have only a short leaf, not reaching above the raceme. The flowers of *P. pumilum* (also confined to the North Island) have a greenish tongue, while the tongue of *P. nudum* is red and is fringed with fine hairs.

Pratia angulata
Panakenake

Lobeliaceae (Lobelia Family)
✔ *m* 7–12mm

A low, hairless or almost hairless plant, with spreading, rooting stems, forming a mat. The rounded leaves (2–12mm long, 2–8mm wide) have entire or coarsely toothed margins. Flower stalks are up to 60mm long, and much longer than the leaves. The corolla tube is split to the base along one side.

It lives in damp places beside streams, under light trees, in grassland, and occasionally on lawns. It flowers from October to April.

The leaves were cooked and eaten by the Maori. The flowers are very similar to those of selliera (*Selliera radicans*) which has anthers fused into a tube around the style, and a distinctive pollen cup surrounding the stigma. It grows in salt marshes and places where water is brackish.

Prunella vulgaris*
Self-heal

Lamiaceae (Mint Family)
✚ 10–15mm

A low perennial, with no smell, which is unusual for members of the Mint Family. The leaves are entire or with shallow teeth. The inflorescence is dense and parallel-sided, with two leaves immediately below the head. The upper lip of the flower is helmet-shaped, and the calyx has two lips, about half as long as the corolla. The corolla is two-lipped, the upper lip hooded, the lower lip three-lobed, with small teeth on the edge of the middle lobe.

Self-heal lives in damp paddocks, lawns and waste land, flowering from November to April.

At one time this plant was used as a cure for sore throats, a condition known as 'brunella'. The more recent name 'prunella' is derived from this.

Also, according to the Doctrine of Signatures (p. 20), it was thought that this plant would heal wounds caused by sharp implements. This idea came about because the flower in profile has the outline of a bill-hook. Some of its early names were sicklewort, hookweed and carpenter's weed.

Pterostylis banksii
Tutukiwi, Common greenhood orchid

Orchidaceae (Orchid Family)
40mm

A low to short perennial, with four to six grass-like, keeled leaves on each plant. The leaves are up to 250mm long and slightly sheathe the stem. Each plant has a single flower, the central sepal being green, helmet-shaped and usually more than 25mm tall. The dark green veins of the central sepal are a distinctive feature. Another feature is that the lateral sepals project sideways from the flower, and have an orangy pink, tail-like appendage, longer than the sepal itself.

It lives on the floor of forests and flowers from October to December.

There are 19 species of *Pterostylis* in New Zealand, of which *P. banksii* is the commonest.

Reseda luteola *   Resedaceae (Mignonette Family)
Wild mignonette, Weld, Dyer's rocket   4–5mm

A medium to tall biennial with narrowly lance-shaped, entire, wavy-edged leaves and a single stem bearing a raceme of green-yellow flowers. The flowers have four sepals and four petals.

It grows in waste areas, beside roads and in gardens, flowering from November to February.

Weld was formerly important for its yellow dye. Common mignonette (*R. odora*) is sometimes grown in gardens for its pleasant perfume. The leaves retain this perfume when dried and, for this reason, the ancient Egyptians placed dried mignonette plants in tombs beside the mummies. When he was fighting in Egypt, Napoleon discovered the plant and sent seeds to Josephine in France, where the plant became popular and soon spread all over Europe. Two other mignonettes frequently occur in New Zealand, each distinguished from *R. luteola* by having at least their upper leaves pinnately lobed. White mignonette (*R. alba*) has white flowers with five or six sepals and petals. Cut-leaved mignonette (*R. lutea*) has yellow flowers with six sepals and petals.

Stachys arvensis *   Lamiaceae (Mint Family)
Staggerweed   ✗ 6–7mm long

A low to medium, hairy annual with no smell. The leaves are oval or rounded, with round-toothed margins, and the upper leaves are unstalked. The corolla is only a little longer than the calyx; the calyx teeth are about as long as the calyx tube. The upper lip of the corolla is small and not hooded, shorter than the lower lip.

It grows in waste areas, gardens, paddocks and beside roads. It flowers throughout the year.

Hedge woundwort (*S. sylvatica* *) is named because of its dark blood-red corolla, which has white markings. It has a strong, unpleasant smell, and is much taller than staggerweed. It is common in the North Island, but is relatively uncommon in the South Island.

Trifolium arvense*
Haresfoot trefoil

Fabaceae (Pea Family)
3–4mm long

A low to short annual with trefoil leaves, which have narrow, hairy leaflets. The inflorescence is cylindrical in outline. The flowers are white at first, turning pinkish later. The sepals are longer than the petals and have long silky hairs.

It is common in waste areas, coastal areas, on pasture and on cultivated land. It flowers from August to May. The roots of *T. arvense,* like those of most of the Fabaceae, bear irregular swellings, known as root nodules. Inside these live nitrogen-fixing bacteria. These are unusual in being able to take nitrogen from air in the soil and convert it to soluble compounds such as nitrates. The plant is able to absorb these nitrates from the nodules, which means that it can flourish in poor soils deficient in nitrogenous minerals. Farmers grow crops such as clover so that, when the roots are ploughed in at the end of the season, the soil is enriched with additional nitrogen.

Trifolium dubium*
Suckling clover

Fabaceae (Pea Family)
2.5–4mm long

A low, prostrate annual with trefoil leaves, the leaflet tips being slightly notched. The middle leaflet has a longer stalk than the other two leaflets. The inflorescence is a rounded head of only 5–20 flowers, and the petals turn brown when dead, just covering the straight pods.

Suckling clover lives in grassy places, including lawns and playing-fields, roadsides and waste ground. It flowers from October to June.

Suckling clover is the commonest of the yellow clovers. At first glance, with its trefoil leaves, it resembles some of the smaller, yellow-flowered oxalis species (p. 67) but, in suckling clover, there are several, small, pea-like flowers in a head, while in oxalis the flowers are regular and solitary. Hop trefoil (*T. campestre**), another yellow-flowered clover, is distinguished from *T. dubium* by the dark red spot on each leaflet. The inflorescence is broadly rounded, and consists of 20–40 flowers.

Trifolium pratense*
Red clover

Fabaceae (Pea Family)
10–16mm long

A short to medium perennial with hairy, trefoil leaves, the leaflets usually with a whitish crescent-shaped mark. The inflorescence is terminal, rounded or ovoid, many-flowered, and very shortly stalked, with two leaves close beneath it. The sepals are hairy, usually half as long as the petals. Occasionally the flowers are cream or white.

Red clover is common in pasture and in cultivated or waste land. It flowers from October to March.

The name 'clover' comes from the Latin *clava*, meaning 'club': the symbol on the clubs suit of playing cards represents the clover leaf. It is widely cultivated as a pasture plant. The phrase 'living in clover' refers to the contentedness of cattle grazing on a paddock of lush clover plants.

Trifolium repens*
White clover

Fabaceae (Pea Family)
8–15mm long

This is a creeping, perennial plant, the stems rooting near the bases of the leaves. The plant is almost completely hairless, with possibly a few hairs on the leaves and calyx. It has trefoil leaves, usually with a whitish crescent on each heart-shaped leaflet, and straight side veins, remaining thin at the leaf margins. Inflorescences are produced in the axils of the leaves, on long stalks; they are rounded and many-flowered.

White clover grows in a wide variety of places, flowering from July to March.

It is grown for pasturage. The strawberry clover (*T. fragiferum**) has the same creeping and rooting habit, but has pale pink flowers. Its leaflets are narrower and have curved side veins that thicken toward the leaf margins. *T. subterraneum**, or subclover, is another white-flowered clover-like plant, but it is hairy and its inflorescences have only two to five flowers of normal size. Smaller, sterile flowers develop later. As the fruits ripen, the flower-stalks curl downward, burying the ripening pods in the soil. The pods are turned back as the inflorescence touches the soil. At the same time, the calyxes of the sterile flowers enlarge, anchoring the seed-pods in the soil.

Verbena bonariensis*
Purple-top

Verbenaceae (Verbena Family)
3mm

A tall, erect perennial, its stems square with bristly hairs on the angles. The leaf base has two lobes, partly clasping the stem. Flowers are small with five pink-purple petals, joined to form a narrow tube. The flowers are arranged in dense spikes up to 30mm long, at the top of the plant. The spikes do not elongate appreciably at fruiting.

Purple-top lives on roadsides and in other open waste areas, also in pastures. It flowers from January to June.

Its species name means 'from Buenos Aires', the city in South America. A related, though less common, species is *V. brasiliensis**, from Brazil; the margins of its leaves taper gradually to the point of attachment to the stem, instead of being lobed.

Verbena litoralis*
Blue vervain

Verbenaceae (Verbena Family)
2–3mm

A tall, square-stemmed perennial, with a rough feeling on the angles of the stem. The leaves are mostly stalked, except the upper ones. They are lance-shaped to rhomboid, toothed, and with sharp hairs. The spikes become longer (more than 50mm long) as the flowers develop, and the flowers are not as densely packed as in purple-top. They elongate to 150mm long at fruiting.

It grows on roadsides and track-sides and other open waste areas, especially near the coast. It flowers all through the year.

Vervain (*V. officinalis**) is similar, but has pinnate or pinnately lobed leaves and spikes up to 150mm long at maximum flowering, and 250mm long at fruiting. Many mysterious and magical uses for vervain were recorded in the past. It was used by the ancient Druids in their ceremonies, for cleansing the altars of the Romans, as a prevention of witchcraft and to prevent dreaming. More practical uses are found for lemon verbena, which provides the verbena oil used to perfume soaps and toilet waters.

105

*Veronica arvensis**   Scrophulariaceae (Foxglove Family)
Field speedwell   2mm

A low to short, hairy, usually erect annual. The leaves are oval to rounded, irregularly toothed and short-stalked. The inflorescence is a dense, leafy, terminal raceme. In the inflorescence, the leaves are short-stalked, and are narrower and simpler than those toward the base of the plant. The petals are blue, and shorter than the sepals. The two stamens jut out on either side of the single style; this is a feature of all speedwell flowers.

Field speedwell is very common in open, modified habitats from sea level to1000m. It flowers from July to April.

The speedwell flowers are characterised by apparently having only four petals, while most other members of the Foxglove Family have five. There are in fact five petals present but the two upper ones are fused together to form a single, but slightly larger, upper petal.

*Veronica persica**   Scrophulariaceae (Foxglove Family)
Scrambling speedwell   10–15mm

A low, curly-haired, prostrate annual with short-stalked, heart-shaped leaves. The flowers are solitary, on long stalks in the axils of the leaves. The dark-veined, sky-blue flowers, with a usually white lower petal, distinguish this from other speedwells.

It is very common on open modified areas and flowers all the year round.

The species originally lived in Persia from where it was collected, and grown in the botanic garden at Karlsruhe, in Germany. About 1805 it escaped and within a few decades it spread throughout Europe. Later, it spread to most other parts of the world, and now it is the commonest speedwell in New Zealand. On warm mornings, when the flower is more likely to be visited by pollinating insects, the filaments of the stamens spread well apart, taking the anthers away from the stigma. On damper, cooler mornings, the filaments do not diverge so widely; the anthers are then closer to the stigma, making self-pollination easier.

Veronica serpyllifolia *
Turf speedwell

Scrophulariaceae (Foxglove Family)
8mm

A low, mat-forming, almost hairless perennial with short-stalked or unstalked, almost entire, oval leaves. The flowers are solitary on stalks almost equal to the leaves. The pale blue or white flowers, with purple veins, distinguish this from other speedwells.

It lives in damp situations, such as wet, grassy areas and around lakes and streams. It flowers all the year round.

The Foxglove Family is a large and varied one, with about 3000 species. It is subdivided into a number of distinct types (tribes). Many species, including the foxglove itself, have irregular flowers, several of which appear in that section. *Veronica* is one of the genera with more or less regular flowers, at least in the shape and size of the petals. Although there are no native veronicas in New Zealand, the tribe to which *Veronica* belongs is well represented here by the closely related genus *Hebe* (p. 58).

Vicia sativa *
Common vetch

Fabaceae (Pea Family)
10–30mm long

A short to medium annual with pinnate leaves ending in tendrils. The leaves have four to eight pairs of oval to narrowly oval leaflets. There is usually a dark spot on the stipules. There are one to two flowers on very short stalks in the axils of the leaves. The calyx teeth are more or less equal in length. They may be longer than, the same length as, or shorter than the calyx tube. Flowers may also be reddish purple, rose, pink or white.

Common vetch lives in waste and cultivated places, inland or on the coast. It flowers from August to June.

The vetches have thin, weak stems, but gain support by climbing or scrambling over other vegetation. Their leaves are pinnate, usually with many pairs of leaflets. The terminal leaflet, and sometimes the pair or pairs of leaflets nearest the leaf tip, are modified as thin, twining tendrils. These curl around any object with which they come into contact, helping to support the plant.

Vicia tetrasperma*
Smooth tare

Fabaceae (Pea Family)
4–8mm long

A short to medium annual with slender, angular stems and pinnate leaves. There are two to five pairs of narrowly oval leaflets, which may be arranged alternately on the leaf stalk as shown in the photograph. It has an inflorescence of one to three flowers on a long stalk. The pods have only four (rarely five) seeds.

It lives in waste and cultivated places, and flowers from October to May.

Another small vetch, but with dull white or pale blue flowers, is *V. hirsuta**, the hairy vetch. The description refers to the hairy pods, for in spite of its common name the stem and leaves of this plant may be completely hairless. There are five to nine pairs of narrow leaflets, and the inflorescence is a raceme of three to seven flowers on a long, leafless stalk.

Viola cunninghamii
Viola

Violaceae (Violet Family)
10–20mm

A low to short perennial with no stem, the leaves and flower-stalks arising directly from a many-headed rootstock. The leaves are broadly oval on long (20–100mm), flat leaf-stalks; the leaf margin is cut straight across at the base, or tapers gradually into the leaf-stalk. The margin has 5–10 very shallow, rounded teeth on each side. The sepals each have a short green 'flap' attached to the base. The lower petal has a shallow pocket, or spur.

Viola lives in damp sites from sea level to 1800m, and flowers from December to March.

The two other native violets have leafy stems. Like *V cunninghamii*, their flowers are white, with purple veins. *V. filicaulis* has a creeping, rooting stem and rounded to kidney-shaped leaves on leaf-stalks 10–20mm long. *V. lyalli* has a prostrate stem with heart-shaped to kidney-shaped leaves on stalks 20–50mm long. Although this family is well known for its ornamental violets and pansies, its only plant of economic importance is *V. odorata*, from which oils used in perfumes and flavourings are obtained.

Index of common names

Acknowledgements

There are seven authors without whose works we should never have been able to undertake or complete this book. These are the authors of the four official floras of New Zealand:

Allan, H. H., *Flora of New Zealand*, Volume I, 1961.
Moore, L. B., and Edgar, E., *Flora of New Zealand*, Volume II, 1976.
Healy, A. J. and Edgar, E., *Flora of New Zealand*, Volume III, 1980.
Webb, C. J., Sykes, W. R., and Garnock-Jones, P. J., *Flora of New Zealand*, Volume IV, 1988.

The first three volumes listed above are published by the Government Printer, Wellington, and the fourth by the Botany Division of DSIR, Christchurch. As well as these, we have made reference to the works of the following authors:

Addison, Josephine, *The Illustrated Plant Lore*, Guild Publishing, London, 1985
Dahlgren, R. M. T., Clifford, H. T., and Yeo, P. F., *The Families of Monocotyledons*, Springer-Verlag, Berlin, 1985
Fitter, Richard, Fitter, Alistair, and Blamey, Marjorie, *The Wild Flowers of Britain and Northern Europe*, 4th Edition, Collins, London, 1985
Genders, Roy, *The Scented Wild Flowers of Britain*, Collins, London, 1971
Gordon, Lesley, *Poorman's Nosegay*, Collins and Harvill Press, London, 1973
Mark, A. F., and Adams, Nancy M., *New Zealand Alpine Plants,* 2nd Edition, Reed Methuen, Auckland, 1986
Martin, W. Keble, *The Concise British Flora in Colour*, Rainbird, London, 1965
Moore, L. B., and Irwin, J. B., *The Oxford Book of New Zealand Plants,* Oxford University Press, Auckland, 1978
Salmon, John, *Alpine Plants of New Zealand*, 2nd Edition, Collins, Auckland, 1985

We would also like to thank Newmans Rentals Limited, Auckland, for providing us with a camper-van in which to undertake some of our searches for plants.

Photographic notes

Kodachrome 64 and 25 films were used throughout. Photographs were taken on an Olympus OM2 camera fitted with a 50mm or 80mm Zuiko macro lens.

Understanding Technical Words

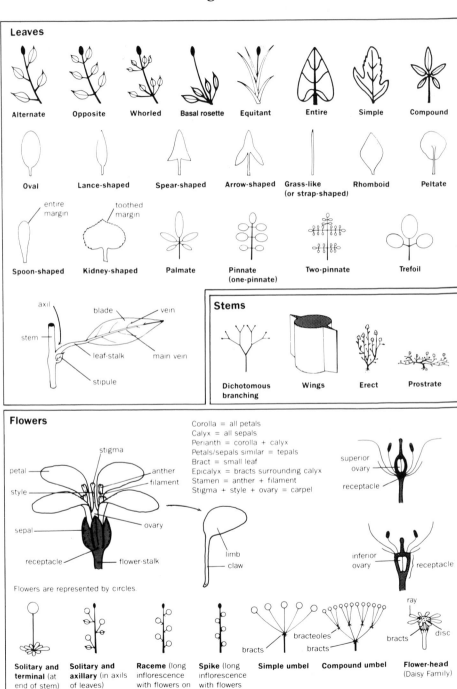

Leaves

Alternate   Opposite   Whorled   Basal rosette   Equitant   Entire   Simple   Compound

Oval   Lance-shaped   Spear-shaped   Arrow-shaped   Grass-like (or strap-shaped)   Rhomboid   Peltate

Spoon-shaped   Kidney-shaped   Palmate   Pinnate (one-pinnate)   Two-pinnate   Trefoil

entire margin   toothed margin

axil   blade   vein   stem   leaf-stalk   main vein   stipule

Stems

Dichotomous branching   Wings   Erect   Prostrate

Flowers

stigma   petal   anther   filament   style   ovary   sepal   receptacle   flower-stalk

Corolla = all petals
Calyx = all sepals
Perianth = corolla + calyx
Petals/sepals similar = tepals
Bract = small leaf
Epicalyx = bracts surrounding calyx
Stamen = anther + filament
Stigma + style + ovary = carpel

superior ovary   receptacle

inferior ovary   receptacle

limb   claw

Flowers are represented by circles.

bracteoles   bracts   bracts   bracts   ray   disc

Solitary and terminal (at end of stem)   **Solitary and axillary** (in axils of leaves)   **Raceme** (long inflorescence with flowers on stalks)   **Spike** (long inflorescence with flowers unstalked)   **Simple umbel**   **Compound umbel**   **Flower-head** (Daisy Family)